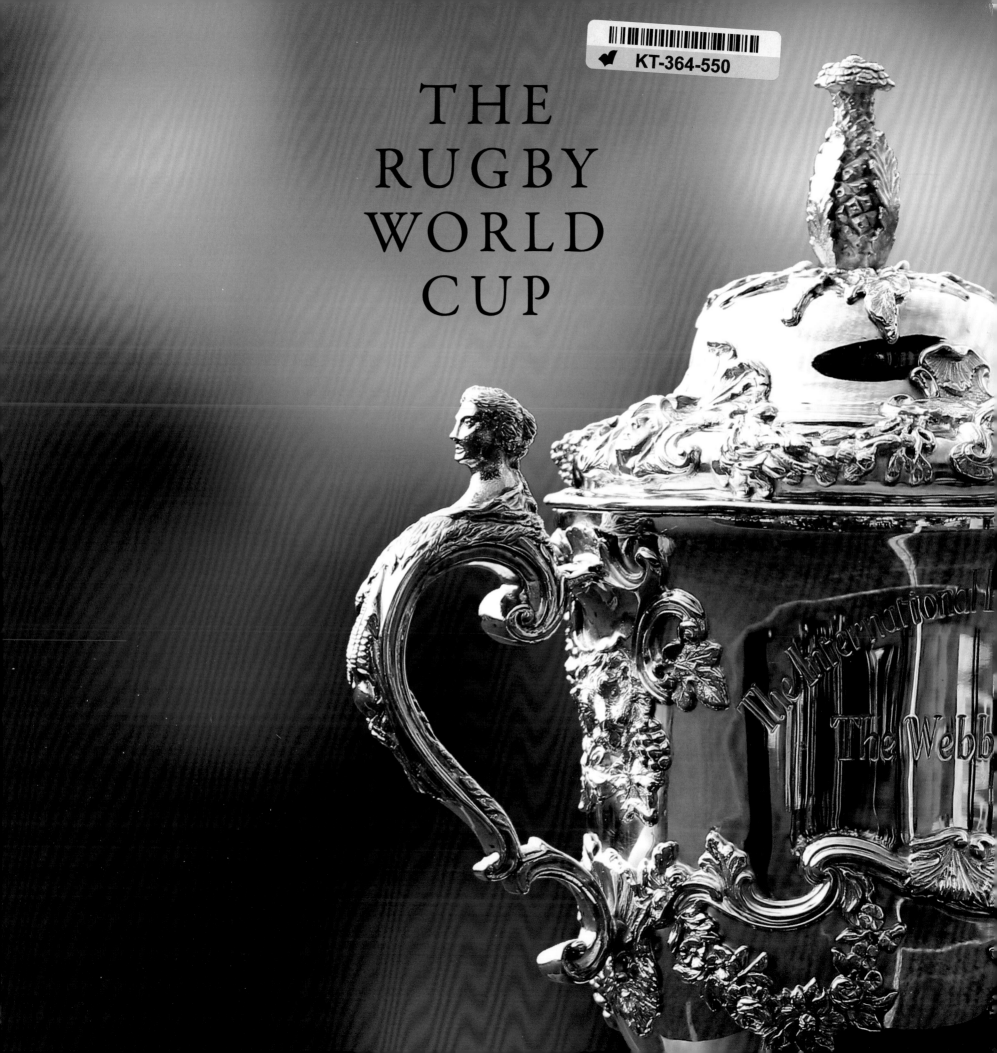

THE RUGBY WORLD CUP

BLOOMSBURY SPORT
An imprint of Bloomsbury Publishing Plc

50 Bedford Square   1385 Broadway
London   New York
WC1B 3DP   NY 10018
UK   USA

www.bloomsbury.com

BLOOMSBURY and the Diana logo are
trademarks of Bloomsbury Publishing Plc
First published 2015
© Brendan Gallagher 2015

British Library Cataloguing-in-Publication Data
A catalogue record for this book is available
from the British Library.

ISBN HB: 9781472912626
ePDF: 9781472912633
ePub: 9781472912640

2 4 6 8 10 9 7 5 3 1

Designed by Austin Taylor
Printed and bound in China by
C&C Offset Printing Co.

Bloomsbury Publishing Plc makes every effort to
ensure that the papers used in the manufacture
of our books are natural, recyclable products
made from wood grown in well-managed forests.
Our manufacturing processes conform to the
environmental regulations of the country of origin.

To find out more about our authors and books visit
www.bloomsbury.com. Here you will find extracts,
author interviews, details of forthcoming events
and the option to sign up for our newsletters.

BRENDAN
GALLAGHER

THE
RUGBY
WORLD CUP

THE DEFINITIVE PHOTOGRAPHIC HISTORY

BLOOMSBURY

Contents

Foreword

IT IS IMPOSSIBLE to play elite sport without wanting to prove yourself the best, which is why we have World Cups.

As a rugby player in the late 70s and early 80s I was extremely proud to represent England and the Lions but agonisingly the inaugural Rugby World Cup in 1987 came just a few years too late for me. I used to look around a little enviously at football, cricket, rugby league, basketball and hockey, which had their own World Cups while every other sport boasted its own 'Everest' at the Olympics every four years. But not Rugby Union.

It was a yawning gap in Rugby Union's make-up. One year, 1981, I was lucky enough to be a member of the Barbarians squad that won the Hong Kong Sevens, which had quickly emerged as a wonderful, almost riotous, celebration of the global game that hinted massively at what might be if Rugby Union could only shake off its old entrenched attitudes.

Thanks to a number of visionaries, who recognised rugby union's sporting and commercial needs, that gap was eventually filled in New Zealand in 1987. It started modestly but from that small acorn a mighty oak has grown. Rugby World Cup is now a phenomenal sporting occasion, the commercial powerhouse of the game and a vital four yearly staging post in rugby's evolution.

This book captures and records that ongoing journey pictorially. The rugby and the characters; the blood, sweat and beers; the courage and humour; the picturesque rural grounds enjoying their day in the limelight and the great stadia of the modern sporting world filled to overflowing. For many players a World Cup is where they tearfully say farewell to the sport they love while for others, such as Jonah Lomu, it is the occasion when they joyously announce themselves. World Cups are an emotional roller-coaster.

Rugby World Cups are not easy to win. No team has yet won back-to-back tournaments. New Zealand needed six attempts after 1987 before they won again in 2011 and our victory with England in 2003 only came after the painful lessons of 1999 and a massive concerted effort to become the number one team in the world in between times.

When you are present at a World Cup your primary focus must be the rugby itself, and your team's performance, but you can't help but get caught up in the tournament itself. Supporters from all countries make their presence known and happily rugby's special brotherhood ensures that the vibe is always friendly and good-humoured.

In the week before the 2003 Final I had no hesitation in encouraging the England squad to relax and chill in the cafes and restaurants around our Manly Hotel, to mix

with the fans, and feed off their passion and energy. I was constantly amazed at the sheer number of travelling England fans by the way – the sea of white flags and shirts as we ran out to warm up against Australia took my breath away and still brings a lump to my throat.

Having lived in Australia for six years I loved the way that great sporting nation got behind the 2003 World Cup, especially the smaller teams, and contrary to what some people think I also relished the 'banter' shall we call it with the local media.

We were quickly dubbed 'Dad's Army' which made me smile because I knew for a certain fact that physically England would outlast any team in the tournament. 'Is that all you've got?' read one of the headlines after our pretty convincing pool victory over South Africa – which was the moment I knew for sure we had the Aussies rattled. It was all good fun though and after the final the Aussie press were generous in their praise as was Eddie Jones and his Australia team.

Rugby World Cups can transcend the sport itself.

The ultimate expression of that is clearly South Africa 1995 but even in 2003 it was an extraordinary moment when 750,000 people packed into central London for our victory parade. There was a massive feeling of communal unity. November 22nd 2003 is a day, one way or another, that we can all share for the rest of our lives and the only event that comes close in that respect is London 2012.

I've never tired of hearing all the stories of where various England fans watched that 2003 final around the globe and how they spent the weekend celebrating. It sounds like we missed quite a party although I can assure you it was pretty lively in Sydney as well

So enjoy this book, not only for the wonderful images and memories laid out in front of you but for the personal memories and recollections I know it will also inspire.

Clive Woodward
MAY 2015

Origins of the Rugby World Cup

The Rugby World Cup has become such a part of the global sporting landscape, ranking third only to the Olympics and the Football World Cup in terms of viewing figures and commercial revenue, that its belated and seemingly rather random birth as recently as 1987 seems mystifying. If it was such a great idea, and manifestly ticks so many boxes, why was rugby union the last major team sport on the planet to organise a world championship?

The same old problem

To find the answer to that you need not stray too far from the old and bitter argument that once existed in rugby union's ranks about professionalism. The history books will show that rugby union turned 'open' – i.e. professional – on 26 August 1995 at a landmark meeting of the International Rugby Board (IRB) in Paris, but de facto the game was set on an inevitable path toward professionalism the moment New Zealand kicked off the opening game of the inaugural World Cup against Italy in 1987.

Staging a World Cup would inevitably involve harnessing all the commercial forces that existed in the hitherto amateur game and 'going to market' and selling the product to TV and media outlets. It entailed attracting sponsors, and very quickly it would need a full-time professional secretariat to cope with the logistics and maximise profit margins at the sport's showpiece occasion. How could you possibly have all that new money and those resources pouring into the game and not reward, or even offer basic recompense, the star athletes involved without whom the competition would be stillborn? Of course you couldn't, as many of rugby's elder statesmen privately and fearfully realised. Entrenched in their amateur ethos and their very particular view of the game, they fought off the very notion of a World Cup for as long as possible, realising that once the genie was out of the bottle there could be no going back.

Perhaps if the original Olympic rugby experiment had been better founded it might have been different, there could have been an honourable 'amateur' alternative, but that petered out disappointingly in Paris in 1924, ignored and unsupported by rugby's big hitters. Retrospectively it still seems strange that the most 'amateur' of games – the favourite sport of Baron de Coubertin who refereed France's first international rugby match – should refuse to engage properly at the top table

previous pages: **Reaching for the stars:** England's Wade Dooley – aka the Blackpool Tower – contests a line-out with Australia's Rod McCall and John Eales in the 1991 World Cup Final at Twickenham.

◀ **For nearly a century** the pinnacle of the game had been a Lions tour of South Africa or New Zealand. But that, by definition, was the preserve of the old elite. What about the rest of the rugby world?

▶ **Rugby fans started looking enviously** as the Cricket World Cup went from strength to strength. Why couldn't rugby have such a competition? Here the crowd spills onto the famous Lord's turf at the end of the 1983 final

of amateur sport, but rugby union was going down its own idiosyncratic path. The annual Five Nations tournament became rugby's core 'international' competition, augmented by occasional high-profile tours of the Home Unions and France by New Zealand, South Africa and Australia. The international scene was very exclusive and inward looking, with the only variation to the above being the British and Irish Lions tours to those southern hemisphere giants. For decades the status quo went unchallenged.

Even during those years rugby was played, but not particularly encouraged, in many other nations, such as Argentina, Germany, Japan, Canada, USA, Romania and the Pacific Islands. In terms of rugby governance, however, those 'lesser' rugby nations were ruthlessly excluded from the inner circle and their developmental needs were ignored. For decades they had no voice on the IRB Council, which consisted entirely of the Five Nations, New Zealand, South Africa and Australia. Long term, it was a recipe for stagnation and decline, but for decades those in power sought mainly to protect the exclusivity of 'their' club and failed to see the bigger picture.

The tide begins to turn

One or two visionaries popped up occasionally to bravely suggest a global competition along the lines of football's World Cup, which proved an immediate success when it was introduced in 1930. Former Australia international Harold Tolhurst, who later became a Test referee, and Manly stalwart Jock Kelleher made themselves unpopular in the 1960s by suggesting that rugby follow football's lead with a World Cup. They irritated those in power to the extent that the IRB circulated a memo to member nations in 1968 reiterating their opposition to any such competition.

It is difficult now to understand the mindset of those involved, but in fairness they were of an era and were convinced they were protecting a game they considered to be very special. By way of illustration, here is an extract from an article written by Wavell Wakefield in 1971 for the publication *Touchdown*. As a former captain of England, President of the RFU and an IRB board member, Wakefield was a fully paid up member of the inner circle and here he comments about a World Congress the RFU had organised to celebrate its centenary:

'There could even be a World Cup for Rugby though I for one hope it does not happen. The Rugby Union made it clear that the main object of its World Congress was to show how the game is played, and conducted, in England. That means an amateur game, played for recreation and enjoyment by people who spend the rest of the week at work.

'A World Cup is quite enough of an ordeal for our soccer players whose living it is. For amateur rugby players it would introduce a much too demanding complication into their daily lives. If every country approached the game as we do it might be a different matter. But these are days when sport is so often used as a vehicle for political propaganda, there is the problem of countries withdrawing from this or that world sporting event for political reasons. Rather than become involved in that kind of thing I would prefer to see our own rugby revert to its time honoured domestic format with as few commitments outside of the British Isles as possible.'

As few commitments outside the British Isles as possible? Ouch! Such archaic and xenophobic views from one so well placed and powerful didn't seem to augur well for the game, but nonetheless the tide did begin to turn. The success of the early Cricket World Cups – hosted by England in 1975, 1979 and 1983 – excited the sporting public who started asking, reasonably enough, where was rugby union's equivalent? In 1982, the PR man Neil Durden-Smith, representing International Sports Marketing (ISM) presented a detailed proposal to the IRB as to how a Rugby World

Cup might work, but again it did not find favour. Bill Mclaughlin, a former president of the Australian Rugby Union, was impressed by the project and suggested that a World Cup competition be organised in 1988 to celebrate the Bicentenary of the Australian nation, although that idea in turn was quashed by his board.

Other factors were coming into play, however. In New Zealand, the rugby authorities were getting twitchy at the interest and support shown for the country's football team reaching the World Cup finals in 1982. Where was the equivalent outlet for New Zealand's pride and joy – the All Blacks – to flex their muscles and bring honour and glory to the nation? Meanwhile, in the cut-throat world of Australian sport, which seems to throw up more than its fair share of entrepreneurs, David Lord caused a panic with his plans to sign up the world's top 200 rugby union players

professionally. He intended to launch a travelling eight national World Rugby Circuit (WRC) not dissimilar in concept to that Kerry Packer had used to revolutionise professional cricket in 1977 although, lacking the backing of such a hard-driving media mogul, the project quickly faltered and disappeared.

Next to up the ante was France, where a quasi-professional scene had existed at club level for many years. This had attracted a Nelsonian eye from the IRB, who felt investigating and proving the actuality of payments to or rewarding of players was impractical and turned a blind eye. The French tabled a formal proposal to the IRB in 1984 that a World Cup be held at some future date, and the IRB finally buckled to the extent of asking Australia and New Zealand to undertake a feasibility study. The two unions looked at a crowded sporting itinerary and concluded that the last week of

▶ John Kendall Carpenter
was one of the prime movers and shakers in making Rugby's World Cup dreams become a reality.

◀ The annual sevens
tournament at the old Hong Kong Stadium opened the eyes of many. Rugby was played across the globe and not just in the old IRB founder member nations. The game deserved, and needed, a global showpiece

May and the first three weeks of June 1987 was the only practical window. Working back from that date meant the tournament had effectively to be approved by the IRB's Annual Board meeting of March 1985, so suddenly the pressure was on. New Zealand manager Dick Littlejohn and former Australian captain Sir Nicholas Shehadie were tasked with undertaking the feasibility study and then presenting the idea to all eight of the IRB founder members.

The politics began in earnest. In the strictly non-democratic world of rugby that then existed, England, Ireland, Wales, France, Scotland, New Zealand, Australia and South Africa all had two votes on the board, while the rest of the world had no say whatsoever. Ironically, South Africa, was banned at that time from playing all international rugby because of apartheid. However, they were firmly in favour of a World Cup and, although their votes were temporarily suspended, the South Africans were still a powerful voice in the smoke-filled rooms where the crucial decisions were taken.

The horse-trading continued. South Africa, with Danie Craven always their leading voice, would happily support the New Zealand and Australia bid, but on the understanding that as soon as South Africa were readmitted to the international fold the IRB would look kindly in their direction when it came to the staging of future World Cups. Even in 1985, it seems there was an acknowledgement by some that eventually, one day soon, apartheid would be toppled and South Africa would cease to be an international pariah.

Craven is often portrayed as a hard-core Afrikaner, but he saw the changing picture and a little further down the line it was he who outraged many in 1988 by arranging talks with the ANC in Harare to discuss the setting up of a multi-ethnic South African Rugby Union.

France, meanwhile, had decided to come down in favour of a World Cup after their wily president Albert Ferrasse secured an understanding that teams from the FIRA organisation that he chaired – the likes of Romania, Russia, Italy – would not be excluded from any World Cup.

For a while it seemed like the 'nos' still had it. The four Home Unions (8 votes) appeared to be against a World Cup, while unequivocally in favour were Australia, New Zealand and France (6 votes). South Africa were also in favour, but temporarily disenfranchised.

It was close enough for the lobbying to continue, however, and Shehadie was convinced that his old rugby playing mate from England, John Kendall-Carpenter, was ready to break ranks along with Keith Rowlands from Wales. After all, there was nothing in the rules that said that the two delegates from one nation had to vote the same way.

That was the situation when the IRB, meeting in Paris on 21 March 1985, decided to take a break from negotiations and went for an afternoon's river cruise to clear their heads before reconvening to take the final vote that night. When the result of that 'secret' vote was finally revealed, it was 8-6 in favour of a World Cup; the assumption was that Kendall-Carpenter and Rowlands had indeed switched at the last moment, as Shehadie had always thought possible. The 1987 World Cup, rather against the odds, was going to happen and an Englishman, John Kendall-Carpenter, was appointed chairman of the organising committee. For a while at least, the talking had stopped. It was time for action.

1987

'At the beginning it had been so rough on a lot of those players they wouldn't go downtown with anything that identified them as All Blacks in case they got abused. But, by the end of the tournament they were very proud to walk down the street and be acknowledged. That shows how the New Zealand public changed because of the type of rugby we played.'

Sir Brian Lochore

▼ **Allez Les Bleus, et les blancs et les rouges.** The French squad in patriotic mode ahead of the first World Cup. How many famous names can you identify? Backrow L to R : Dominique Erbani, Jean-Luc Joinel, Eric Champ, Francis Haget, Alain Carminati, Jean Condom, Alain Lorieux, Laurent Rodriguez. Middle row : Guy Laporte, Louis Armary, Jean-Baptiste Lafond, Franck Mesnel, Jean-Pierre Romeu, Serge Blanco, Philippe Sella, Eric Bonneval, Alain Estève, Patrice Lagisquet. Front: Rodolphe Modin, Philippe Bérot, Jean-Pierre Garuet, Pierre Berbizier, Jacques Fouroux (coach) Daniel Dubroca, Denis Charvet, Pascal Ondarts, Jean-Louis Tolot, Philippe Dintrans.

Previous pages. **This is for you guys.** The New Zealand nation had fallen out of love with the All Blacks following their controversial Cavaliers tour to South Africa in 1986. Skipper Dave Kirk and his team rectified that by winning the inaugural World Cup.

New Zealand and Australia

The truth is that in the still largely amateur world of rugby union there were very different perceptions of what the 1987 World Cup actually constituted, which was in many ways reflected by the close vote that had established the competition in the first place. Was it a tournament or was it really just an extension of the normal summer tours most teams embarked on? Was it, in fact, a festive gala occasion, a sort of 15-a-side version of the Hong Kong Sevens? Was it a one-off or was it here to stay? The chairman of the organising committee itself, John Kendall-Carpenter, admitted it was all a bit ad hoc and an 'experiment'. A sponsor, Japanese communications company KDD, was found less than a month before the competition and the host TV broadcaster deal was only signed in the bowels of Eden Park half an hour before the opening game between New Zealand and Italy. This was belt and braces stuff, but some of man's best inventions often are.

On the pitch, New Zealand and Australia were certainly in deadly earnest. They had led the lobbying for the World Cup and, along with France, were possibly the furthest down the route to quasi 'professionalism'. The Wallabies needed to fight their corner in a hectic domestic market awash with world-class sports, while New Zealand craved a bigger stage for the All Blacks. In all three countries, star players seemed to appear quite frequently on TV advertisements and one assumes they weren't lending their names to products entirely for free.

Having lost a home series to Australia in 1986 and been beaten 16-3 by France in Nantes later that year, the All Blacks had embarked on a big clearout of players and a tactical rethink with much more emphasis on attack. They had pressed so hard for a World Cup it was imperative, in their minds, that they won it. With the tournament fast approaching, they sent many of their most likely players on a short spring tour of England and Wales in the guise of a New Zealand Barbarians XV that routed all concerned, putting 60 points on the board against a strong Barbarians team at the Arms Park.

As for the rest of the teams, well, let's just say that perhaps it wasn't quite so intense. England's hooker Brian Moore explains: 'We just didn't understand what you had to do to play in a

▲ **The opening ceremony** of the inaugural Rugby World Cup was not a lavish affair!

tournament, and if other teams are honest, I suspect they might say the same. Only the Kiwis were flat out in tournament mode. We didn't know whether it was going to be a success or a complete turkey. We had never played in a tournament other than the Five Nations and even then you went home after the game and only played every two weeks, in fact, sometimes there was a month between matches.

'There have been some exaggerated comments about our approach out there, it wasn't over the top at all, but we did still have tour courts, a couple of good old-style nights out and a kickback day on a boat, that sort of thing. It was "amateurish" in every sense of the word, but then again we had all taken our annual holiday to be there. Absolutely nobody knew what the World Cup was going to grow into. The criticism of our approach has been mainly retrospective. We also spent the entire time in Australia, where the tournament had very little profile. The main event was definitely happening over in New Zealand and we didn't feel part of it. We were operating on the fringes of a tournament we didn't really understand.'

One of the initial problems had been who to invite exactly. The eight founder members of the IRB, minus South Africa who were still banned because of apartheid, were obviously the first names on the list and the organisers cast around for other teams who could join their party. Romania had been very strong in the early 1980s, indeed they might well have reached the latter stages had a tournament been held in 1983, so they received an invite along with Russia, who promptly turned it down, reportedly because of South Africa's continuing position of power on the IRB committee despite their ban from playing. That doesn't quite ring true and, following close on the mass boycotts of the 1980 and 1984 Olympics, Russia's withdrawal probably owed much more to the general tit-for-tat Cold War politics of the time. Eventually, additional invites were sent out and accepted by Japan, USA, Canada, Tonga, Fiji, Argentina, Italy, Zimbabwe and the Romanians. Strangely, Western Samoa, for no good reason that anybody can remember, were overlooked.

After a relatively lean spell by their own standards, the pressure was very much on New Zealand, especially after the unofficial, and unsuccessful, New Zealand Cavaliers tour of South Africa the previous year had alienated large sections of their rugby public, which effectively meant *the* entire nation. Many in New Zealand thought it totally unacceptable for the All Blacks to

◀ **Brian Lochore** was more than a legendary New Zealand captain and coach to the 1987 All Blacks. He was their guiding light and realised the importance of getting the public back on side.

▶ **Wade Dooley** in charge for England in their 34–6 pool victory over USA in Sydney. Not exactly a full house!

provide succour to the apartheid regime and doubly so if, as was widely rumoured, the New Zealand players were being lavishly rewarded by South African backers for their efforts. All the players involved received a two-match Test ban on their return, which derailed a number of Test careers, but a good percentage were still involved in the 1987 World Cup squad. There was a hangover, though. Unthinkably, as the World Cup got under way, the All Blacks seemed to be on trial and had lost the public's affection.

New Zealand did, however, have one massive factor in their favour, the timely appointment as coach of Sir Brian Lochore – that rare creature, a legendary player who was just as good a coach and manager. Unflappable, relaxed but always on the ball and at the cutting edge of playing trends, Lochore was the ideal man to first calm nerves and then inspire. As the squad assembled early in May, Lochore took stock and liked what he saw: 'They were in great nick and were the fittest team there by a considerable margin, but they'd done it themselves. They hadn't been chased around the paddock by trainers.'

And then came a charm offensive to win back the public. 'At the beginning it had been so rough on a lot of those players they wouldn't go downtown with anything that identified them as All Blacks in case they got abused. But, by the end of the tournament they were very proud to walk down the street and be acknowledged. That shows how the New Zealand public changed because of the type of rugby we played.'

Perhaps one pivotal moment came when Lochore decided there needed to be a closer connection still with New Zealand's rugby heartland and arranged for the squad to spend a day 'going bush' out in rural Wairarapa, where all the players would also be billeted out for the night. 'I wanted them to go for two nights, really mix with the families and communities, but they were a little uneasy, so I made it one,' recalls Lochore ruefully. 'They rode horses, they rode motorbikes, they went shooting and fishing and then, when we got on the bus to go back to Wellington, just about in unison they said, "Why couldn't we stay two nights?" My answer isn't repeatable.'

Kirwan gets the blood up

To further the connection, New Zealand decided to take their pool games around the country, playing in Auckland, Christchurch and Wellington, and starting with an emphatic 70-6 win over Italy at a half-empty Eden Park where, initially at least, curiosity rather than excitement was the prevailing mood. That is until the moment that ignited the World Cup for evermore, a wonder try by New Zealand's strapping right wing John Kirwan, who sprinted and zigzagged his way for 80 yards past eight or nine Italian defenders for possibly the most spectacular individual try ever seen in Test rugby. Later, Kirwan compared the try to a training run he used to do in an Auckland park, where he would jog to the top of a hill and then sprint back down, slaloming between the young fenced-off trees that had recently been planted.

The All Blacks displayed a pace and precision rarely seen before and also unearthed a new star in the form of flanker Michael Jones, who had been capped by Samoa in 1986 against Wales but had quickly been recruited by New Zealand, as was allowed in those days. Full-back John Gallagher, London born and bred before moving to Wellington to become a policeman, was another rising star. Frankly, New Zealand seemed a class apart from the first whistle and romped through their pool with embarrassing ease, beating Fiji 74-13 and Argentina 46-15.

◀ **New Zealand skipper Dave Kirk** was devastating on the break for New Zealand. Here he takes on Fiji's Elia Rokowailoa in the All Blacks' crushing 74–13 pool match win over Fiji.

▶ **France's full-back Serge Blanco** was a unique and maverick talent but his basics were absolutely textbook. Adrian Stoop himself would have purred at his passing technique in this pool game against Scotland.

Lochore's exciting side quickly won back the New Zealand public's support and provided the main narrative of the tournament. Elsewhere, it was a bit more evenly contested. France and Scotland grappled for supremacy in Pool 4 and, appropriately enough, fought out a 20-20 draw when they met, while Wales took Pool 2, beating runners-up Ireland 13-6 in the decisive match. Over the Tasman Sea, neither Australia nor England were troubled by Japan or the USA, and it was the Aussies who took the pool courtesy of a 19-6 win over England at the Concord Oval, which did admittedly include an absolute howler of a decision when David Campese was awarded a try after a comically blatant knock-on.

So, on to the quarter-finals, which were a mixed bag to say the least. Wales' 16-3 win over England at Ballymore is often cited as one of the worst World Cup games in history by winners and losers alike. A bad-tempered scrap on a sapping quagmire of a pitch, it came soon after a spectacularly violent Five Nations encounter between the two teams. As Moore recalls: 'I pity anybody who had to sit through that match. Awful. That pitch in Brisbane was like semi-bog, it drained everything out of you, it was a rubbish game, we played very badly and they played slightly less badly. But it was a watershed moment. I sat in the changing room afterwards and thought – in fact I didn't just think, I told everybody in earshot – that if we were going to put in all this effort it was absolutely pointless turning up and playing like that. If nothing else, the 1987 World Cup made us realise that England rugby had to change. We had to move forward.'

In the other quarter-finals, New Zealand at last encountered meaningful resistance at Lancaster Park, Christchurch, before dispensing with Scotland 30-3, but scoring only two tries in the

process. France defeated Fiji 31-16 in an entertaining romp at Eden Park, and Australia were convincing 33-15 winners over Ireland in a rugged game in Sydney.

WEBB ELLIS ARRIVES ON THE SCENE

All of which set the scene for the first truly classic match of the tournament, the semi-final between France and Australia in front of a fairly sparse 17,768 crowd at the Concord Oval Sydney. The pictures, however, were beamed around the world as two of the most naturally gifted and free flowing of teams laid on an attacking extravaganza. Playing catch-up, France won 30-24, thanks to a last-minute try from the heavily bandaged Serge Blanco who seemed on the point of expiring as he plunged over for the decisive score. New Zealand, meanwhile, had produced probably their best performance of the entire World Cup in dismantling Wales 49-6. They looked completely dominant in an eight-try blitz at Ballymore that set up the inaugural final.

For the final, a capacity 48,035 squeezed into Eden Park where there was a tangible big match atmosphere. The action was a little nervy, with New Zealand reaching half time 9-0 up following a converted try by Michael Jones and a Grant Fox penalty. But after

◀ **New Zealand skipper Dave Kirk** was devastating on the break for New Zealand. Here he scores in spectacular fashion in the All Blacks' crushing 74–13 pool match win over Fiji.

the break, New Zealand relaxed and put the game beyond doubt with tries by Kirwan and skipper Dave Kirk to seal a convincing 29-9 win. The trophy, picked up that day by Kirk and squad captain Andy Dalton, was a fine sight, although true to the character of the 1987 tournament it had been acquired in something of a rush. A couple of weeks before the competition started, John Kendall-Carpenter reminded the organising committee that they didn't have a trophy. He was immediately dispatched to Garrard, the Crown jewellers in London, to view the stock of available trophies in their vaults. One particular trophy took his eye – a 1906 silver gilt, gold-covered cup made by Carrington & Co., based on a design by the famous Huguenot silversmith Paul de Lamerie, one of the top craftsmen in the first half of the 18th century. The asking price was £6,000, and frankly RWC was not in a position to barter. The Webb Ellis trophy was thus pressed into service.

As the dust of the inaugural World Cup settled, New Zealand hooker Sean Fitzpatrick recalls its last day at Eden Park: 'The final itself was a wonderful occasion. To play at your home ground, in your home town, in front of a capacity stadium on an awesome spring afternoon – it doesn't get a lot better than that. And to play against the French made it all the bigger. Our game against them late in 1986 [sometimes known as 'the Battle of Nantes'] had seen a number of incidents after France resorted to some pretty heavy-handed tactics – so this was our opportunity for a bit of payback.

'Did I enjoy the match itself? Probably not. I enjoyed it a lot more once the whistle went and it was over. The celebrations were

actually pretty tame, though. For us, it was a case of job done – a job that was expected of us – and now let's move on to the next thing, which was a game against Australia in a few weeks. We went back to the hotel, had one or two drinks in the hotel bar and were in bed by one or two in the morning. You have to remember: we were amateurs, so most of us were back to work on Monday. Our wing Craig Green tells a great story about how we won the Rugby World Cup on the Saturday and at 5 a.m. on Monday he was standing on a corner in Christchurch with his packed lunchbox, waiting to go roofing. There was no real big party parade. It was just another win for the All Blacks really.'

Going into the 1987 World Cup there was no assumption that the competition would be continued and its future was only assured at the IRB's annual meeting in March 1988, which also resulted in the appointment later that year of a full time professional secretariat headed by Keith Rowlands, and also including chairman John Kendall-Carpenter, Marcel Martin (France) and Russ Thomas (New Zealand). The IRB also received a 90-page debrief on the 1987 tournament, which recorded a working profit of $1.95 million and also made the very strong recommendation, given the dislocations caused by hosting the tournament in New Zealand and Australia, that all future competitions be staged in just one country. Wise heads nodded in agreement at the manifest sagacity of such a suggestion ... before those same wise heads rubber-stamped plans to hold the 1991 tournament in FIVE countries! But that's another story.

▼ **A study in concentration.** Michael Lynagh lines up a penalty shot in Australia's 19–6 pool victory over England. The great Wallaby was to amass 195 points during his World Cup career, which ended in South Africa eight years later.

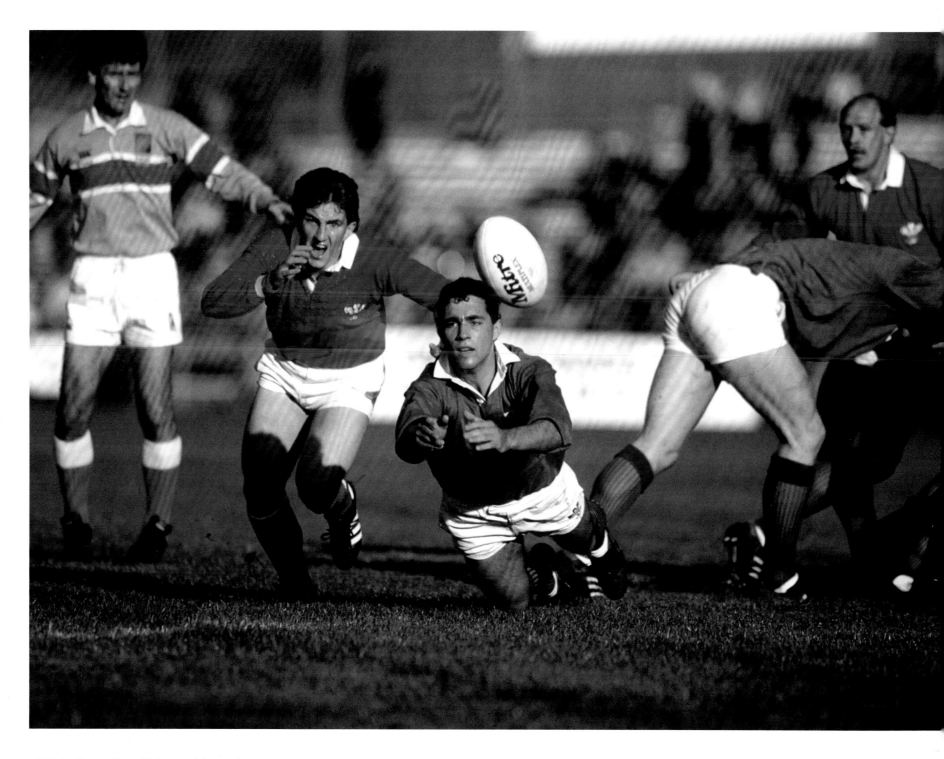

◀ **Right from the off** the World Cup gloried in taking matches to smaller venues. In 1987 Palmerston North enjoyed hosting Wales' pool game against Tonga. The Welsh in unfamiliar green, ran out 29–16 winners.

▲ **Ireland's Michael Bradley** and Wales scrum-half Robert Jones were old rivals... but locking horns 12,000 miles away in Wellington New Zealand was a novelty. Wales won their pool game 13–6.

▼ **The multi-talented Zinzan Brooke** made his World Cup debut against Argentina at Wellington Park. His impact was immediate and he rounded off a fine performance with a try but even he couldn't force his way into the All Blacks' back row for the knock out stages.

▶ **The old Athletic Park Wellington** was not the place for those who suffer with vertigo. The main stand on the right was reputed to have the steepest seats of any rugby stadia in the world. None of which deterred a packed house for New Zealand's pool match against the Pumas.

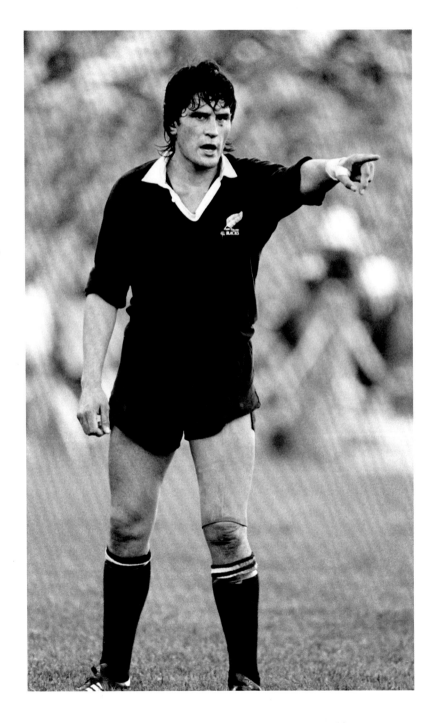

▲ **A sceptical England** weren't sure if the first World Cup was an end of season jolly or a cut-throat tournament here to stay. Generally, they didn't impress but they did cut loose against Japan with skipper Mike Harrison scoring three of their ten tries in a commanding 60–7 win in Sydney.

▶ **John Jeffrey rejoiced** in the nickname of the 'Great White Shark' and showed no mercy as Scotland defeated Zimbabwe 60–20 in their pool game.

Quarter-finals

▼ **Ireland flanker Phil Matthews** works up a head of steam against Australia but to no avail. The Irish went down 33–15 in their quarter-final against France.

▲ **Rugby union didn't get to see** enough of Jonathan Davies in his pomp before he 'went North' but he was an influential member of their first ever World Cup. Wales' 16–3 quarter-final win over England on a gluepot of a ground in Brisbane wasn't a classic but his class shone through nonetheless.

▲ **Bleddyn Bowen,** a policeman with the South Wales Constabulary, was an underrated player, his subtle skills providing the perfect foil to John Devereux in the Wales midfield.

Semi-finals

▼ **Australia, with young guns** like scrum-half Nick Farr-Jones to the fore, had impressed in their pool games and against Ireland in the quarter-final and went into their semi-final against France in Sydney as strong favourites. Farr-Jones, though, was a marked man and here tries to give France flanker Eric Champ the slip.

◀ **Blanco was a sublime attacking player** but Australia were not the first or last team to believe he might be vulnerable under the high ball. Predictably, a couple of early 'bombs' were launched in his direction early in their semi-final. Aussie wing Peter Grigg is contesting the ball on this occasion.

▲ **History will show** that France's last ditch 30–24 win over Australia was the making of the World Cup as a tournament. A modest crowd of 17,768 attended the Concord Oval but TV fans worldwide lapped up a staggering game of sublime quality and much excitement, which ended up with Serge Blanco evading both Tommy Lawton and the touchline to claim a last-minute winner in the corner. The World Cup was here to stay.

▲ **Wales' blockbusting centre John Devereux** steams in for Wales' solitary try in their 49–6 semi-final defeat against New Zealand. Devereux was another star Welsh player who was eventually lured to Rugby League, joining Widnes in 1989.

◄ **New Zealand may have possessed** some of the most lethal backs on the planet but it all starts up front in big-time Cup rugby. Step forward a mighty front row, namely tight head John Drake, hooker Sean Fitzpatrick and loose head Steve McDowell.

▼ **With proud Maori Wayne 'Buck' Shelford** a massive influence in their squad, New Zealand really started to crank up their haka routine at the 1987 World Cup. Wales on the receiving end this time.

◄ **Steve Sutton and Richard Moriarty** gain a rare line-out success in their quarter-final hammering against New Zealand. The match was done and dusted at half-time with New Zealand leading 27–0 but the dismissal of lock Huw Richards in the first minute after the break was the final straw. The second half was a long haul for Welsh players and spectators alike.

The
Final

▶ **New Zealand knew that Serge Blanco was the man** who could light the touch paper for France and were determined to give him no space. Wayne Shelford clatters in.

◀ **Twelve months before the World Cup** Michael Jones had made his Test debut for Western Samoa against Wales. But the brilliant flanker was dual qualified and New Zealand coveted his lethal mix of pace, strength and aggression as openside flanker. He ticked all their boxes and before long he was New Zealand's linchpin, probably the stand-out performer of the entire tournament.

◀ **Londoner John Gallagher** emigrated to New Zealand to become a police officer in Wellington. He ended up as the All Blacks, full-back and a World Cup winner.

▶ **France lock Jean Condom** tussles for the ball as a packed crowd at Eden Park looks on. The World Cup had started with half-empty stadia but was the hottest ticket in town a month later.

▼ **John Kirwan evades Philippe Sella** to score. Kirwan was one of the most lethal try scorers the game has ever seen, scoring 35 in 63 Tests for New Zealand.

▼ Bittersweet moment? Hooker Andy Dalton had seemed set to captain the All Blacks at the World Cup but was sidelined with injury so Kirk took over.

▼ Dave Kirk is presented with the William Webb Ellis Cup. New Zealand's captain was to play just one more game for New Zealand, a Bledisloe Cup game against Australia in Sydney, before enrolling at Oxford University and heading for a career in politics and business. He is now an Australian citizen.

▶ New Zealand's victorious team met for a 20th anniversary lunch in 2007 and were presented with a caricature team group.

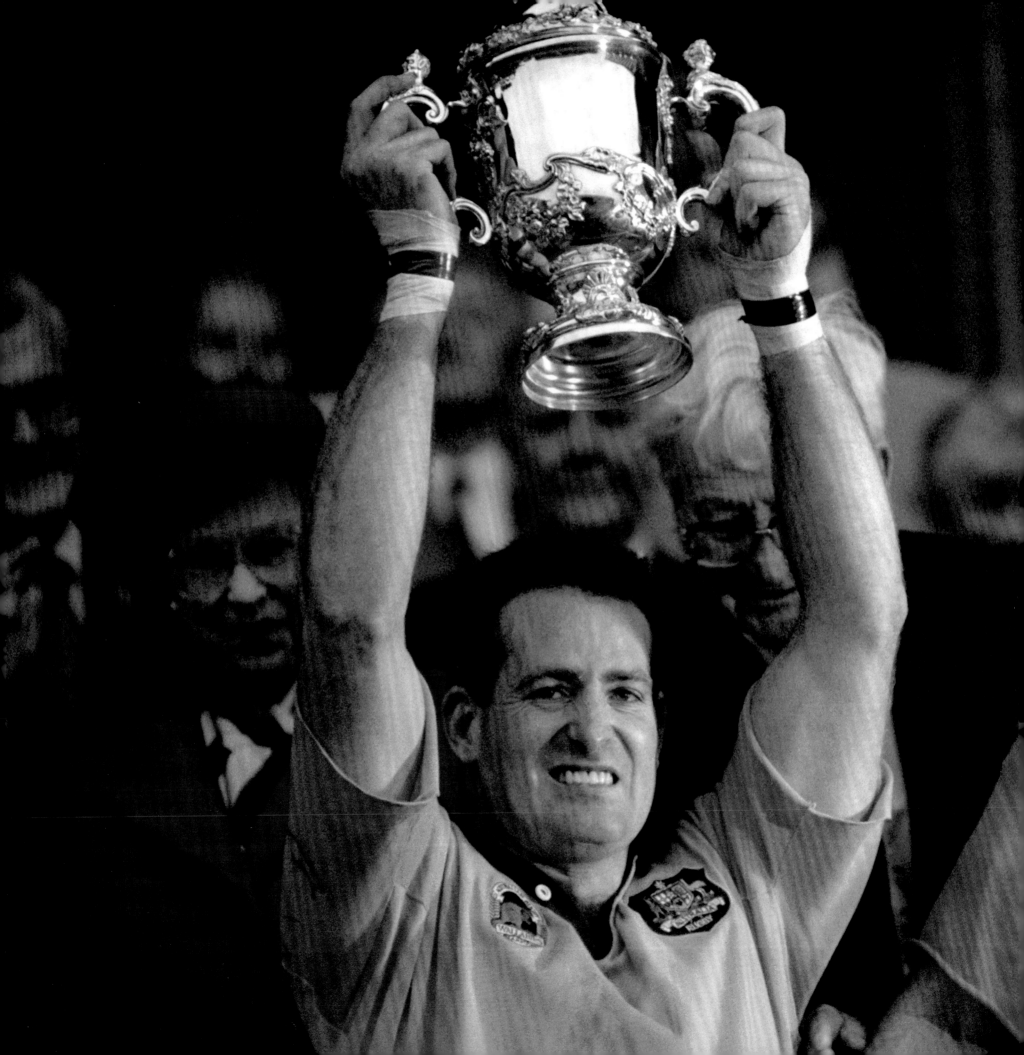

1991

‘We might have tweaked our tactics on the hoof, but the bottom line was that it made no difference, Australia were better than us. We have to look at ourselves and admit that if we had played that same Aussie team ten times they would have beaten us on seven of those occasions. They were an outstanding unit.’

Will Carling

2 England, Scotland, Wales, Ireland and France

So where were we? Having received and applauded the official report on the 1987 World Cup, which strongly recommended that all future World Cups be held in one country, the IRB promptly voted that the 1991 tournament would actually be held in the Four Home Unions and France. Five rugby nations, three sovereign states. Given rugby's endless politics and horse-trading, that decision was not entirely surprising and such was the momentum of the new tournament that it didn't prove ruinous, although it did establish the template for a strangely unsatisfying Five Nations-based World Cup in 1999. Back in 1991, the split decision probably started with the determination of France's Albert Ferrasse – whose support, lobbying and vote had been important in 1987 – to secure a significant part of the action for his extremely powerful federation. There was a debt of sorts to repay to France by the southern hemisphere nations and realistically nothing was going to happen at a northern hemisphere-based tournament in 1991 without a French-based pool and two quarter-finals. That political victory was in turn the catalyst for all the Home Unions wanting to host their own games. The result was seemingly a mishmash of a competition featuring 19 different grounds. It seemed like a recipe for chaos and indeed, on some occasions, very nearly was. As with Australia in 1987, the French segment of the tournament seemed completely self-contained and divorced from the main competition and, except for an explosive quarter-final against England, the atmosphere and ambience was disappointing.

▲ **By 1991 the tournament was attracting Royal Patronge.** HRH Prince Edward declares the tournament open at Twickenham before England's game against New Zealand.

And yet despite everything the 1991 World Cup was a major success, and marked the moment that rugby union truly arrived on the world scene. The basic precept of the competition was manifestly sound; it so obviously filled a need for players and fans and commercially the sport began to flex its muscles. On-site attendances increased from 600,000 to 1 million and the cumulative TV audience rocketed from a reported 300 million to 1.4 billion. The revenue from all sources increased from £3.3 million in 1987 to £23.6 million in 1991 with a profit of £4.1 million as opposed to the £1 million reported in 1987. Judiciously held in the autumn, thus avoiding any clash with summer sports and slotting into the calendar before football took its normal grip, the competition's media profile was massive and England's advance to the final added an extra element. Rugby was now appearing on the front pages as well as the back, with individuals being picked out for praise and lionisation and their profiles rising exponentially. The advertising revenues came pouring in and sponsors started forming a queue for future tournaments, which, of course, in many ways confirmed the worst fears of those who suspected a World Cup would lead inevitably to professionalism. They were absolutely right.

In 1987, the competition had been by invite only and, although the number of nations who could contemplate playing in a World Cup was still strictly limited, this time there was a qualifying tournament of sorts. The eight quarter-finalists from New Zealand in 1987 were waved through automatically, while the remaining eight spots were taken after 25 teams contested in four regional tournaments.

Western Samoa won their way through a Pacific tournament, which also saw Japan and Tonga advance, while Korea were unsuccessful. Italy and Romania emerged from a European zone, which also included Holland and Spain, while in Africa – with South Africa still excluded – Zimbabwe earned the one available place ahead of Morocco, Ivory Coast and Tunisia, who nevertheless enjoyed a welcome taste of genuine international tournament rugby. In the Americas, it was basically a seeding competition with Canada, Argentina and USA all going through in that order.

'Good job we didn't play the whole of Samoa'

And so to the competition proper and without doubt the 'story' of the pool rounds was the emergence of Western Samoa, who qualified for the quarter-finals at the expense of Wales, beating them 16-13 in a game of high tension at the Arms Park. The Samoans were an explosive, eclectic mix of players either born and raised on the island or born into Samoan families in New Zealand. The moot point is that the vast majority of the squad had plenty of experience of tough New Zealand club and provincial rugby and were more than capable of holding their own at the highest level. Samoa was a colony of New Zealand until 1962 and that close relationship was confusing, with many players possessing dual nationality. Michael Jones, star of the 1987 tournament for New Zealand, had made his Test debut for Samoa only the previous season while, after the 1991 tournament, standout players Frank

◄ **Ball coming in ... now.**
England's rise to prominence in the early 90s was firmly based on their powerful pack.

Bunce and Stephen Bachop switched to New Zealand. Pat Lam, Samoa's No. 8 in 1991, was briefly tempted by the New Zealand pathway, but then changed his mind and subsequently captained Samoa at the 1995 and 1999 World Cups. Va'aiga Tuigamala played for New Zealand in 1991, but appeared at the 1999 World Cup for Samoa.

In 1991, Western Samoa were a formidable team. In addition to those already mentioned, Brian Lima was a fast and destructive player famed for his tackling, hence the nickname 'chiropractor' because he rearranged opponent's bones! To'o Vaega was one of the silkiest centres in world rugby and had been sought by New Zealand since he made his debut in 1986, while Matt Keenan was a feisty lock, Junior Paramore was a class back-rower and Apollo Perelini, who later became a rugby league player of some repute, was a force of nature in the pack.

Their day of all days came on 6 October when they provided a rugby spectacle and an 'upset' story that instantly became an important staging post in the tournament's development. Wales were staggered – physically and metaphorically – by the Samoans' strength and power, and quickly lost two key players to injury in line-out ace Phil May and flanker Richie Collins. It was a tight game and although the early 1990s were not vintage years for Wales, this was not a case of the side capitulating – they were narrowly beaten on the day by an outstanding team.

And Wales were a tad unlucky. The splendid To'o Vaega may have deserved a try for his efforts, but to most eyes Wales scrum-half Robert Jones won the race with the Samoa centre in the 42nd minute when both sought to touch the ball down. French referee Patrick Robin disagreed, and the score was crucial, as Samoa forged ahead and built a 13-3 lead. Although Wales hit back later in the half, a penalty by scrum-half Matthew Vaea saw Samoa home. After the match To'o Vaega, whose wife had given birth to a son less than two weeks earlier back in Samoa, announced that the boy would be called Cardiff – who has since gone on to become a very useful provincial player in New Zealand. Meanwhile, a gallows humour set in around the pubs of Cardiff. 'Western Samoa? Good job we didn't play the whole of Samoa,' the Welsh fans muttered as they stared into their beer.

Something that is often forgotten is that slightly less than 72 hours later Samoa went to the well again in dreadful muddy conditions and torrential rain at Pontypool Park. In a performance that possibly even surpassed their efforts at the Arms Park, they

lost 9-3 to eventual world champions Australia in a game where they enjoyed very little luck. Samoa had announced their arrival in style.

Australia at the death

In Pool 1, New Zealand had won the opening day game against England as those two emerged as quarter-finalists. Many rugby aficionados insist the best moment from that pool came when Italy's scrum-half, Ivan Francescato, sidestepped his way through the USA defence for a cracking try at Otley, surely one of the most picturesque World Cup venues ever. Sadly, Francescato was to die prematurely, aged just 32, suffering a heart attack one evening after he had appeared for his beloved Treviso in an Italian club match. Scotland and Ireland predictably progressed from Pool 2, although there were a number of memorable moments from the free-running, quick-handling Japanese, including a peach of a first-half try by their prop and former captain Toshiyuki Hayashi. Another score in the second half, from Katsuhiro Masuto after a superb break from Yoshihito Yoshida, was the try of the tournament for many.

Pool 4 in France was largely uninspiring fare except for growing evidence that Canada, with a strong pack and the big boot of Gareth Rees, had forged the strongest side in their history. The 'Canucks' were unlucky in losing 19-13 against France at Agen, but progressed along with the French to the knockout stages.

The quarter-finals produced three of the best World Cup games yet seen. At the Parc des Princes, England won an explosive and particularly physical match against the French 19-10, a volatile encounter coming just six months after the two sides had met in a memorable Six Nations Grand Slam decider. Tensions were predictably high. England, with their mean-machine pack, planned on getting their retaliation in first and an early assault on the revered Blanco, as he gathered a high ball and was thrown around like a rag doll, still makes the hairs on the back of your neck stand up. France possessed a brutish pack at the time, but England matched them all the way.

With the score poised at 10-10 going into the final quarter, France were pressing for the try that would possibly have opened the floodgates. A scrum-five was awarded and France were rock steady on their put-in, setting it up perfectly for Marc Cécillon, a 6ft 4in rock from Bourgoin. At that point, however, Mick 'the Munch' Skinner entered the fray, reading the situation perfectly and timing his bone-shattering tackle to the millisecond as Cécillon momentarily gathered himself before surging for glory. But there was more. It wasn't that Skinner merely stopped the Frenchman stone dead, he then proceeded to drive him back fully 5 yards, dismissing the Frenchman from his very presence, much to the delight of the 20,000 travelling England fans. The siege had been lifted, and from that moment you knew with certainty that nothing was going to stop England.

Skinner was on a high and the French nonplussed. The maverick Eric Champ – old mad eyes himself – clearly wanted to punch the Munch into the next parish but, in a rare moment of discipline, opted for a strange staring competition as the two went head-to-head, literally. Skinner won that little stand off as well. After the game the French completely lost it and coach Daniel Dubroca attacked New Zealand referee David Bishop in the tunnel. Despite protesting his innocence, Dubroca resigned soon afterwards.

In the rain of Lille, New Zealand were made to work uncommonly hard by the Canadians, some of whose forwards, such as Gord MacKinnon, Al Charron, Glen Ennis and Norm Hadley, were fast becoming players of world repute. New Zealand eventually prevailed 29-13, but they were a long way from being the dominant force of 1987. Western Samoa finally ran out of steam at Murrayfield, losing 28-6 to Scotland who cleverly met fire with fire by sending Gavin Hastings crashing into their defence at every opportunity. That left Ireland to play Australia in the remaining quarter-final at Lansdowne Road.

An already exciting match ramped up another notch with four minutes to go when Ulster flanker Gordon Hamilton sprinted 40 yards, holding off David Campese to score and give Ireland an 18-14 lead. A nation held its breath and began to dream; a semi-final against a faltering New Zealand seemed in their grasp, a place in the final itself could even be a possibility and surely they would have nothing to fear against either Scotland or England. But then, at the death, Australia refused to be part of the Irish dream and rescued the situation with a 79th minute score for Michael Lynagh.

THE BUSINESS END

Having enjoyed a relaxed week in Dublin, Australia then stormed into the final with a convincing 16-6 win over New Zealand at Lansdowne Road, a match notable for a brilliant individual try by Campese, who arrowed across the field at an acute angle to outstrip the All Blacks' defence. The magical Australian wing then

made a score for Tim Horan with a sensational over the shoulder, no-look pass, straight from the Hong Kong Sevens, a tournament he graced for much of the 1980s and 1990s.

The second semi-final was an entirely different affair, a tense war of attrition between old enemies. At 6-6 deep in the second half, Gavin Hastings had a penalty in front of the posts to nudge Scotland

into the lead. To general shock, somehow he contrived to miss it. Moments later, England worked their way upfield and Rob Andrew kicked a short-range drop goal to ease England into the final.

'I had been tackled heavily by Micky Skinner just previously and he didn't mess around,' recalls Hastings. 'The physio came on to the field and was using the cold sponge on me. I wasn't fit to take the kick and clearly – with hindsight – I should have asked Craig Chalmers, who was a high quality kicker, to take over. I learned a lot about myself that day though. The fact I went on to captain the Lions and lead Scotland and, hopefully, continued to play in a positive fashion, is testament to what drove me on as a rugby player and it sometimes annoys me that people might only remember me for that miss.'

The day of the final, England captain Will Carling was photographed draped in a St George's Cross flag on the front page of the *Sun*, the world's biggest circulation newspaper, offering

▶ **Where did it all go wrong?**
Wales' lock Phil May, injured earlier in the match, contemplates an 'unthinkable' 16–13 defeat to Western Samoa.

◀ **The Royals continued to support** the tournament all the way. HRH Princess Diana and Prince Harry were at the Arms Park for Wales' pool match against Australia, who installed themselves as competition favourites with a thumping 34–3 win.

confirmation that the World Cup had really arrived. HM Queen Elizabeth inspected the teams and a curious game unfolded. Australia, with some of the world's most potent attacking players in their ranks, kept it tight and played largely percentage rugby while England, whose formidable pack had bossed the knockout games against France and Scotland, opted for a much wider, more adventurous game. In the end Australia, who scored the solitary try through prop Tony Daly, won 12-6 and Nick Farr-Jones became the second winning captain to lift the Webb Ellis trophy aloft. After which the debates started. Why had England changed their modus operandi?

'We had toured Australia that summer and lost 40-15, and basically our pack got hammered up front and Australia also produced a better kicking game on the day,' recalls Carling. 'We had meetings about this a couple of times in the week before the final and discussed tactics. It was decided we had to open up a

bit, try and stretch Australia. This notion that we just woke up on Saturday morning and decided to change tactics is a complete nonsense. We did try and put tempo into the game and we had the players – but we were inaccurate and didn't make the final pass tell. If we made a mistake at all it was in not realising that our pack had progressed since the summer and were now shaping up much better against the Australians. We might have tweaked our tactics on the hoof, but the bottom line was that it made no difference, Australia were better than us. We have to look at ourselves and admit that if we had played that same Aussie team ten times they would have beaten us on seven of those occasions. They were an outstanding unit. Australia weren't at more than 80 per cent and they still beat us fair and square. I have no issues whatsoever with their win and no real regrets about the 1991 World Cup, not like I have from 1995 when I felt we had a much better side than the one we actually put out there on the field.'

▼ **It's neck and neck** going for the line. Who is going to get the touchdown? Robert Jones of Wales or To'o Vaega of Western Samoa? To'o Vaega got the verdict, although the debate continues to this day.

▲ Car park attendants came in all shapes and sizes down Llanelli way.

▶ The World Cup was beginning to spawn a modest commercial arm by 1991. Believe it or not, some of these are now collectors' items.

Early stages

Scotland's pool game against Ireland at Murrayfield wasn't for the faint-hearted. Derek White leads the charge for the Scots.

Japan were outclassed again the bigger teams but produced a stunning performance in defeating Zimbabwe 52–8 at Ravenhill wher wonderful passing was at the hea of their eight-try haul.

No escape for Mark Ring. Australia's openside Jeff Miller, competing with the likes of Simon Poidevin and Willie Ofahengaue, didn't always get a start for Australia but he was exceptional in their pool victory over Wales.

▼ **Rugby is a game for all shapes and sizes** but Samoa's Stan Toomalatai was only ever going to be a hooker. Stan takes a breather in Samoa's plucky 9–3 defeat in the rain and mud of Pontypool Park.

◀ **Most of the small nations** possessed individuals who would have shone in stronger teams and Zimbabwe scrum-half Andrew Ferreira was definitely one such player.

▲ **'Inga the Winga'** – aka Va'aiga Tuigamala – was a force of nature but even with him blasting holes in the opposition defence New Zealand only beat Italy 31–21 at Welford Road. After a career in the League, he returned to World Cup action in 1999... with Samoa.

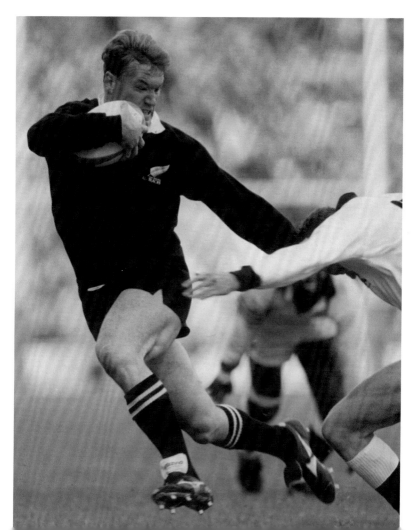

◀ **New Zealand's John Kirwan** was still going strong and proving as elusive as ever. Kirwan seemed to be a sportsman blessed by the Gods but years later, in an acclaimed autobiography, he revealed his life long fight against depression.

Quarter-finals

▶ Are you ready to rumble?
France hard case Marc Cécillon is on charge 5 yards from the England line but has been lined up by Mick 'the Munch' Skinner. Something has got to give. In this case it was Cécillon who was driven back 5 yards by the England flanker in what has been described ever since as 'the tackle'. Inspired by Skinner's defiance, England cleared their lines and won a fractious quarter-final 19–10.

◀ Time for a recuperative tincture?
England had ruthlessly tested the ageing Blanco at full-back throughout their quarter-final. Come the final whistle, Dr Jonathan Webb led the France captain to a place of safety.

▶ It all got a bit hectic in Ireland's memorable quarter-final against Australia. Tim Horan and Simon Poidevin scrag Ireland wing Simon Geoghegan.

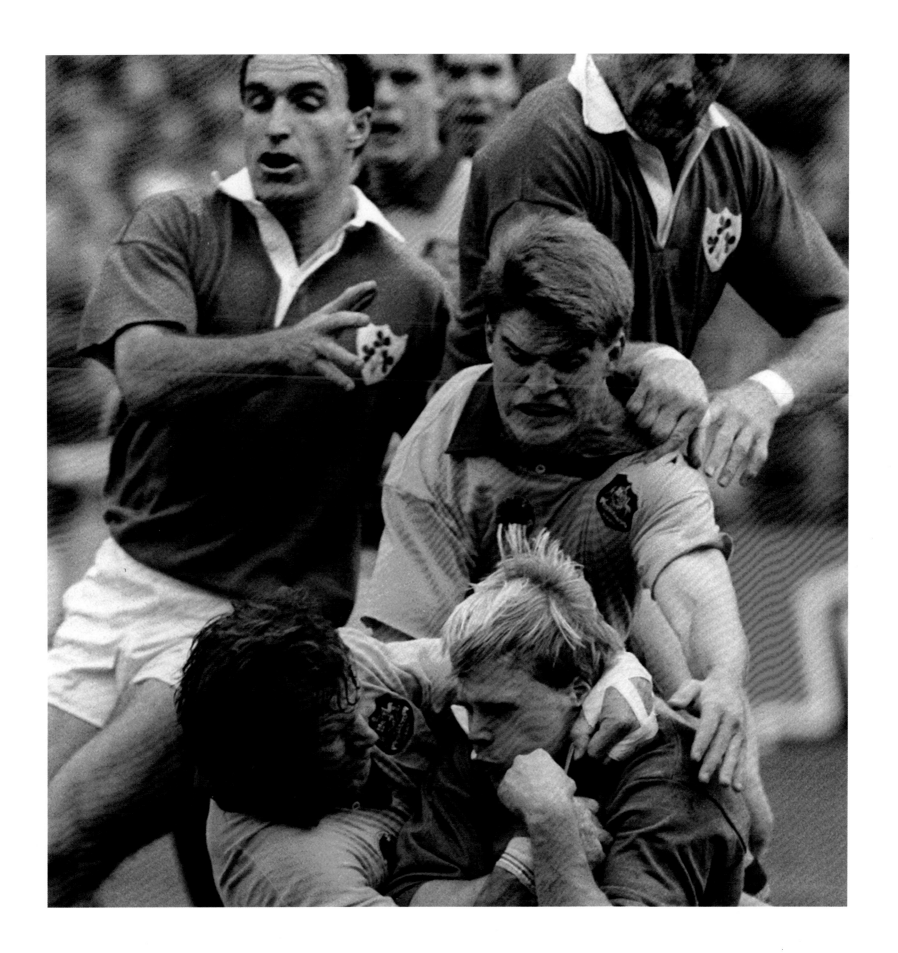

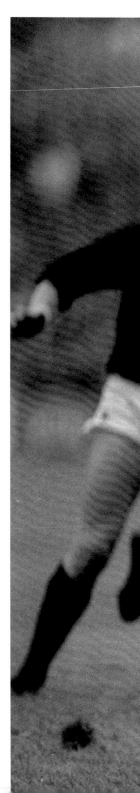

▲ **David Campese was at his zenith in 1991,** both a match winner and a crowd pleaser. Ireland's Brendan Mullin got him this time though.

◄ **Zinzan Brooke tries to escape** the clutches of Canada's exceptional openside flanker Gord MacKinnon, who played two matches for the World XV against New Zealand the following year in Test to celebrate the NZRU Centenary. A fireman for many years, MacKinnon is now a regular world Masters champion at the CrossFit Games.

Semi-finals

▼ **England's tense 9–6 semi-final win** over Scotland was a game of inches. Rob Andrew just clears his lines despite the attention of Scotland scrum-half Gary Armstrong.

▲ **After a convivial week in Dublin,** Australia continued the party against New Zealand in the semi-final with an exhilarating display. Tim Horan steams in for a try after a breathtaking no-look, over the shoulder pass from David Campese.

▶ **Scotland captain Gavin Hastings** can't believe he has missed a penalty in front of the posts, a kick that would have given his team a 9–6 lead. In such a tight game, he immediately sensed it would be costly.

▲ **Scotland prop Paul Burnell** assesses the damage after being caught at the bottom of a ruck in the play-off game against New Zealand.

The
Final

▶ **England felt they needed to offer more** than just forward power to beat such an accomplished side as Australia. In the first half in particular, Will Carling and his backs moved the ball whenever possible but to no avail.

▶ **Blood, sweat and tears.** Full-back Marty Roebuck gave his all for Australia.

◀ **Tim Horan** was a young and fearless new kid on the block in 1991. Brilliant going forward, he also knew the value of a good old-fashioned clearing kick to touch.

◄ **It's Australia's Cup.** David Campese, the player of the tournament, savours the moment.

► **It wasn't to be.** A rueful Will Carling takes his leave after the final. England had lost but rugby's profile had risen tenfold during the World Cup. The game would never be the same.

◄ **The party is underway.** Funny how two hulking great forwards like Phil Kearns and Simon Poidevin get to share a bath while Michael Lynagh enjoys the luxury of one to himself. Life wasn't meant to be fair!

1995

'What our years of engineered division did was to obscure from the mainstream public awareness the fact that rugby was once a thriving and vital sport in many black communities. The history of rugby in black communities actually stretches as far back as that of rugby in white communities. Our coming together as a nation freed us to pool those different histories to the benefit of sport nationally.'

Nelson Mandela

saw the hopes of a newly democratised nation soar. Nothing exemplified
the exhilarating roller coaster of a tournament better than the thunderous
and unexpected pre-match fly-past of a South African Airways Jumbo Jet.
Health and Safety would never allow it these days but inside the cockpit
Captain Laurie Kay deliberately revved the engines and provided
a spectacle that nobody present will ever forget.

Previous pages. **François Pienaar
enjoys the moment.** Outstanding
effort by centre Hennie le Roux to
march around with his 17-stone captain
on his shoulders after extra time. The
Boks were an incredibly fit team.

3

South Africa

Not many sporting events act as the catalyst for a troubled nation to unite under a new flag and leader, witness the birth of a world sporting phenomenon and spark off a fundamental change in the sport concerned, so the legacy of the 1995 World Cup is considerable. The memories of everybody privileged enough to attend are overwhelmingly golden and enduring. No wonder Hollywood swooped some years later and produced an Oscar-nominated film, *Invictus*, based on the tournament and starring Morgan Freeman and Matt Damon.

The core story was deeply political and transcended mere sport. Rugby had always defined the old white 'apartheid' South African culture and to a large extent alienated the vast black majority, so the forthcoming World Cup, with the eyes of the world boring in on South Africa, presented a potentially divisive challenge for Nelson Mandela, who had been elected president in 1992 after 27 years of incarceration.

Huge issues confronted the new Rainbow Nation and many old enmities still raged, but Mandela immediately recognised that it was time for South Africa to present a united front to the world. As the democratically chosen leader of his country it behoved him to make the first move, so from very early on in his presidency he embraced the Springboks, the ultimate symbol of white South African dominance. Through the long lens of history it perhaps seems an obvious move, but at the time it was radical and risky.

Rebirth of a nation

Right from the off – South Africa's return to the international fold in 1992 against Australia in Cape Town – Mandela made a point of attending Springbok home games whenever possible and took to occasionally dropping in on training in his presidential helicopter. At Cabinet meetings he headed off suggestions from ANC colleagues that the famous Springbok emblem was way too symbolic of the bad old days and should be replaced. Mandela would have no truck with that. South Africa was a powerhouse rugby nation and their prowess on the playing field was a source of much pride to a

▲ **Unthinkable just a couple of years earlier.**
Black South Africans cheering their white rugby heroes to the hilt.

significant part of the community. Many members of the black and coloured community were also rugby players, albeit disadvantaged and unheralded. There was a bridge that could be built here. Much better, surely, to be the bigger man, embrace the 'white man's sport', and make the Springboks a source of universal pride. One team one nation.

Despite his previous suffering and humiliation in prison, Mandela increasingly associated himself with the team and formed a close friendship with their new young captain, Francois Pienaar, a powerful blond Afrikaner from Northern Transvaal. The cultural and physical contrast could not have been greater, which is one of the reasons that the images of them sharing ultimate victory together after the final against New Zealand at Ellis Park are so historic – Mandela, the excited fan and father figure wearing his replica No. 6 Springbok shirt, handing the Webb Ellis trophy to a beaming Pienaar. An extraordinary olive branch from the man in South Africa who had most cause to hate everything and anything to do with those who perpetrated the apartheid regime.

'Francois, fantastic support from 63,000 South Africans here today?' SATV anchorman David van der Sandt said, as soon as he could grab the triumphant skipper. Without missing a beat, Pienaar replied: 'David, we didn't have the support of 63,000 South Africans today, we had the support of 42 million South Africans.' The interview was being relayed around the stadium and sparked off the biggest cheer of the day. No wonder Hollywood came calling.

Although a very fine rumbustious flanker, Pienaar would struggle to make an all-time Springboks XV but, more importantly, during this unfolding chapter of history he was an extremely intelligent and eloquent leader in his own right – the right man at the right time. During the previous couple of years and then during the tournament itself he had understood perfectly what was happening to his country and never put a foot wrong. 'The 1995 World Cup became a story about us, the new South Africa finding its identity through sport,' recalls Pienaar. 'June 1995 was the moment in time when the new South Africa took a long hard look in on itself and President Mandela showed the way towards reconciliation by putting his trust in the Springboks. It was a healing process.

'I grew up in apartheid South Africa and as a young kid, when Mr Mandela was a prisoner, the things I heard about him were bad things – sadly so. Around the barbecue fires people would invariably talk about politics and sport and, when the name Nelson Mandela came up, it was accompanied by the words, "terrorist, bad man". When he became president and I got the call to go and see him, you can imagine how nervous I was. I sat outside his office at the Union buildings and I could hear his booming voice, and as he walked towards me the first thing he said to me was in Afrikaans. I tried to switch to English, but he kept steering it back to Afrikaans, so we had an hour's chat, which was very special.

'Before the tournament the South Africa squad were taken to Robben Island and we saw cell 46664 where President Mandela spent so many years. It was an unexpectedly powerful experience and took us all unawares. At one stage I looked over and saw our winger James Small crying his eyes out. I think we probably all shed a few tears that day, but it was a unifying experience.

'On the day of the final, just before we ran out, there was a loud knock on the changing room door and in walked Mr Mandela in a South Africa shirt with a Springbok on his heart. He just said a

quick "good luck boys" and when he turned to go I saw my number was on his back. And that was me gone emotionally, I couldn't sing the anthem because I knew I would cry – I was just so proud to be a South African that day. Afterwards, when I walked up to the podium, Mr Mandela stuck out his hand and said to me, and I still can't believe to this day that he said it, "Thank you Francois for what you have done for this country". I wanted to jump over and give him a hug, but I said to him, "No sir, thank *you* for what *you* have done for this country" because without him telling the ANC and the black community that we were their team, none of this could have happened.'

The last 'amateur' World Cup

Even if you could somehow disregard the startling birth of a nation that was going on before our very eyes, the 1995 World Cup was an epic sporting event and spectacle on so many other levels. Seemingly from nowhere, although those of us attending the Hong Kong Sevens two months earlier had been pre-warned, Jonah Lomu suddenly took the rugby world by storm with a series of

phenomenal displays on the wing that redefined how rugby could be played. At 19 years of age, Lomu was 6 foot 5 inches, 19 stone and, the only time he was recorded for 100 metres, was logged at 10.8 seconds. Much more than that, he was a beautifully balanced runner for a huge man and in those early years, before ill health struck, he was a seemingly irresistible force of nature.

The son of Tongan immigrants living in the suburbs of Auckland, Lomu was like no other rugby player we had ever seen before and with his eye-catching haircut and spectacular tries – he scored seven in total during the tournament and made many more – attracted the attention of many outside of the sport itself. The story goes that Rupert Murdoch caught a glimpse of him early in the tournament and decided that whatever it took, this was a player and a sport that needed to be signed up by News Corp. Low-key meetings with players, administrators and News Corp officials went on throughout the 1995 tournament and on the eve of the final itself came the announcement of the Tri-Nations and 'Super Rugby' Championships by the big three southern hemisphere giants: South Africa, New Zealand and Australia. Rugby union, de facto, had become a professional game even if it took a couple more months before that was formally acknowledged by the IRB at a special meeting in Paris. If a more united South Africa was the great political legacy of 1995, the arrival of professionalism was the sporting legacy. The last 'amateur' World Cup was a huge success on a commercial level and hinted at what was soon to follow. Watched by 1.1 million spectators with a global accumulated TV audience of 2.38 billion, the tournament boasted gross revenue of £30.3 million, yielding a net profit of £17.6 million. The snowball of success was beginning to roll.

Fine margins

As for the rugby, a fast improving New Zealand – determined to give a better account of themselves than in 1991 – started as favourites, even before the emergence of Lomu. A number of other promising newcomers – Andrew Mehrtens and Glen

Osborne – combined forces with enduring legends of the New Zealand game such as Sean Fitzpatrick, Ian Jones, Zinzan Brooke and Jeff Wilson, while former Samoan Frank Bunce was enjoying an Indian summer to his career. The 1995 All Blacks were awesome going forward and cut a swathe all the way to the final. The only question left hanging in the air was what would happen if a team was good enough or brave enough to resist them? For much of the 1995 World Cup the pure rugby narrative – away from the romance and emotion surrounding Mandela's one team one nation – was simple. Who could stop the All Blacks?

For a while, England looked like contenders; under Will Carling they had just claimed their third Grand Slam in five years. But their build-up was thrown into disarray just before the team's departure when Carling's description of the RFU committee as '57 old farts' went down like a lead balloon in the corridors of power at Twickenham. Carling was summarily relieved of his job in a hideous

overreaction. Thankfully, peace talks were initiated and England's most successful captain was reinstated. It was an unnecessary distraction and, coincidence or not, England spluttered their way through the pool stages with workmanlike wins over Argentina, Samoa and Italy. They did, however, find another gear against holders Australia in the quarter-finals when a late drop goal by Rob Andrew clinched a famous and well deserved win in Cape Town, a victory that encouraged much optimism. Just a week later they encountered the nearest thing you will see to a hurricane on a rugby pitch, when Lomu left a trail of devastation in his wake, his four tries helping New Zealand to a commanding 45-29 win and a place in the final.

France are never to be discounted and they fought a campaign of gathering intensity. Tonga and surprise qualifiers Ivory Coast were beaten without fanfare or flourish before they fortuitously squeezed past Scotland in Pretoria with a late try by Émile N'tamack to head the pool and book a quarter-final against Ireland in Durban. The Irish were duly despatched, 36-12. Exactly a week later they were back at the same stadium, Kings Park, but in very different circumstances.

It started raining with biblical intensity on the Friday lunchtime down in Durban and didn't stop for 36 hours. The World Cup semi-final between France and the hosts South Africa was due to kick off the following afternoon, but conditions were appalling. 'With lightning flashing out across the Indian Ocean, thunder echoing round the bay and one end of the ground looking more like a lake than a rugby pitch, there seemed to be no chance of the game starting at all,' wrote Mick Cleary in the *Guardian*.

The World Cup was still evolving as a competition and nobody had ever envisaged a match lost to natural causes. Today it is unthinkable that such a game wouldn't simply be postponed and then re-staged as soon as possible, but back in 1995 the only

stipulation was that in the event of a cancellation the winner would be the team with the best disciplinary record. This presented South Africa with a massive problem because in their bad-tempered pool game against Canada their hooker James Dalton had been sent off along with Canadians Rod Snow and Gareth Rees. If the game in Durban was cancelled, South Africa would be eliminated.

Generally the grounds and facilities in South Africa were world class and streets ahead of anything then existing elsewhere in the rugby world, but Kings Park had never experienced weather like this and was simply not prepared. Remarkably, their front line of defence was a team of five or six cleaners who trooped gamely on to the pitch and began to sweep the stagnant water to the sidelines. It was an extraordinary image in an otherwise cutting-edge tournament – the Springboks' fate seemed to lie in their hands. After a 75-minute delay, referee Derek Bevan took the difficult decision to allow the game to continue. Most of us there

▶ **Numerous problems** confronted the Rainbow Nation on the eve of the 1995 World Cup. Some – many even – predicted chaos and possible violence. Instead, peace and harmony reigned throughout and sport has never been seen as a more effective agent for good.

thought it was probably the wrong call, but to the eternal credit of the French team they made no effort to 'milk the situation' and, with Bevan refeering as sympathetically as he could, there is no question that a proper rugby contest ensued, albeit one of the wettest in history.

South Africa won 19-16 with flanker Ruben Kruger scoring a try and Joel Stransky kicking well, but at the death there was more controversy when massive France lock Abdelatif Benazzi surged for the line and looked certain to score. He was felled by a mighty tackle – it looked like Kruger again, but it was impossible to tell in the rain and mud – and stretched for the line. The French players went up as one to celebrate and the home crowd fell ominously silent, but Bevan ordered no try. There was no TMO technology in those days, but the murky slow-motion replays available suggested that Bevan had, in fact, made the best and bravest call of a very considerable Test career and that Benazzi had been stopped an inch short of the line. Commentators who talk about the 'miracle of South Africa' usually refer to their victory over New Zealand in the final at Ellis Park, but the Springboks were never closer to defeat than against France in the semi-final a week earlier. Fine margins indeed.

Crowning glory

The action moved to Johannesburg for the final. New Zealand were favourites, but not overwhelmingly so in my opinion. They had been absolutely brilliant but largely untested during the previous four and a bit weeks, a scenario that was to trip the All Blacks up more than once in their World Cup history. They had been so outstanding, in fact, that you wondered if they could go to the well one more time. South Africa were battle-hardened and building an unstoppable momentum. There was a tangible feeling that an unlikely Springbok triumph was actually written in the stars. And there was another factor. The one rugby-playing nation who would never be intimidated by a player like Jonah Lomu was South Africa. They knew all about brutal physicality and saw Lomu as a player to target, not to fear. Stop Jonah and there is a very good chance you might stop the All Blacks as well.

And that's exactly what happened. Comparatively lightweight backs like Joost van der Westhuizen and Japie Mulder fearlessly tackled Lomu and held him up until bigger forwards such as Mark Andrews and that man of steel, Kruger, could arrive and add their weight. Lomu was stopped at source; indeed, in eight international appearances he never scored a try against South Africa, one of rugby's more extraordinary statistics.

With Lomu neutered, it became an old-fashioned arm wrestle between bitter rivals and eventually it was a towering extra-time drop goal by Stransky that decided the issue, sparking off hundreds of street parties around the country. Very late that night, outside our hotel in Pretoria, the sight of white South African policemen in uniform dancing with the local black inhabitants until daylight was something that would have been utterly unthinkable even five short weeks earlier.

'I'd love to be 20 again; rugby would be one of my sports. What a game to play and to be a part of,' Mandela said to me during an interview in 2002. 'And the collective memory of this country's rugby will always hold a place of pride for the role it played in nation-building during those first years of our new democracy. Those memorable days in June 1995 when South Africans from all backgrounds and persuasions took to the streets to celebrate a national achievement, commonly embraced, must continue to serve as an inspiration to current and future generations. Rugby players are role models for the youth of our nation and rugby must not allow that beacon event to fade from our memory. Sport reaches people in ways and to an extent that politics and politicians never can.

'What our years of engineered division did was to obscure from the mainstream public awareness the fact that rugby was once a thriving and vital sport in many black communities. The history of rugby in black communities actually stretches as far back as that of rugby in white communities. Our coming together as a nation freed us to pool those different histories to the benefit of sport nationally.'

The film *Invictus* may have condensed a complicated story rather too much for some tastes, but it did capture the feel-good factor of the 1995 World Cup and, of course, the poem itself (written in 1875 by the English poet William Henley) seemed to capture Mandela perfectly. He prevailed and overcame, as did the South Africa side he inspired in 1995.

> *It matters not how strait the gate*
> *How charged with punishments the scroll.*
> *I am the master of my fate:*
> *I am the captain of my soul.*

Build up to the tournament

▽ **It don't mean a thing if you ain't got that swing.** England prop Victor Ubogu was born in Nigeria, Africa was in his blood, and he was quick to join in with the Zulu dancers who greeted England at their Durban hotel.

▲ **There might be a more perfect place** to practise and play rugby than a sunny winter's day in Cape Town. But offhand I can't think of it. David Campese takes five under Table Mountain.

▶ **Australia's Daniel Herbert** never considered himself a frontline kicker but on yet another beautiful Cape Town morning keeping your hand in is a joy.

 **On the eve of the tournament** all 16 teams were flown into Cape Town for a tournament launch dinner. Behind those smiles was a certain amount of terror, with many of the teams experiencing severe turbulence during their flights as South Africa was hit by a huge 'south western', which generated hurricane force winds.

▶ **From small acorns,** mighty oaks do grow. Corporate hospitality and 'village life' was beginning to take a hold in 1995.

▼ **The eyes have it.** Joost van der Westhuizen was at the absolute height of his powers in 1995. A great athlete, undaunted competitor and a very skilful scrum-half indeed.

◀ **Scotland's captain Gavin Hastings** knew he would be retiring the moment his team was knocked out. In the meantime, he was determined to finish on a high and hit the tournament running, in the shape of his life.

▼ **In the 1980s and 1990s** South Africa was way ahead of the other major rugby playing nations in terms of facilities. Kings Park, Durban was one of the many fine stadia that helped make a compelling case for awarding them the World Cup.

▲ **Ireland's call.** The Ireland team had only mastered the words of their new 'overseas' anthem Ireland's Call – written by Phil Coulter – at training the day before their opening game against New Zealand at Ellis Park. But it didn't show. Gary Halpin is lead vocal with good support from Paddy Johns and Gabriel Fulcher.

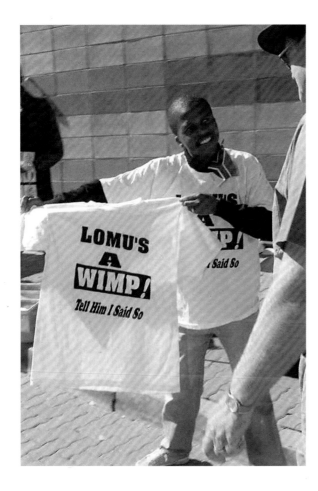

▲ **The street hawkers in Johannesburg** and Rupert Murdoch, it would seem, are not so very different. Both instinctively knew Lomu was box office and there was a few bob to be made.

◀ **Rugby had never seen the likes of Jonah Lomu before.** 6ft 5inches, nearly 19 stone and a 10.8sec man for the 100m. And New Zealand played him on the wing. Lomu appeared to come from another planet. Wayne Proctor (centre) and Gareth Thomas give forlorn chase for Wales at Ellis Park. The linesman is a very distant fourth!

▶ **Prime Argentinian beef** on the hoof. Federico Mendez had switched to hooker by 1995 and enjoyed a fine tournament. All three Pumas' front-row players were voted into the team of the tournament.

Knockout stages

▲ **Thank you and goodnight.** Gavin Hastings is chaired off by Doddie Weir and Rob Wainwright (wearing cap) after Scotland gave it a good rattle against New Zealand in the quarter-final at Loftus

▼ England had disappeared for a two-day break in Sun City straight after their quarter-final win in Cape Town and you wonder if they were quite ready for the intensity of their semi-final against New Zealand back at Newlands. Jonah Lomu lays down the challenge.

▶ Rugby was on the brink of turning professional in June 1995, although the game generally was unaware how imminent that change was. Ostensibly it was still amateur and, World Cup or not, France lock Abdelatif Benazzi needed to catch up with his studies ahead of France's quarter-final with Ireland.

▲ ▶ In retrospect, it is no exaggeration to say that Jonah Lomu was the man who hurried rugby union into professionalism. It was going in that direction anyway, at its own measured pace; but in just over a month in South Africa, Lomu became a global measured sporting icon and figurehead of a sport that clearly now possessed a commercial worth. Lomu's defining moment probably came with his four tries in New Zealand's 45–29 semi-final victory over England when, frankly, he appeared to come

from another planet. Rupert Murdoch is reported to have 'clocked' Lomu in one of his earlier performances and before the match was over was on to his executives at News Corp, insisting that they urgently 'recruit' both the player and the sport. The result, in virtually no time at all, was the creation of SANZAR and the setting up of the Tri-Nations and Super Rugby competitions, details of which were announced to the media at a jaw-dropping press conference on the day before the World Cup Final.

The Final

▼ **Chester Williams was the only man** who came close to upstaging Jonah Lomu. The only player of colour in the South Africa squad, he was forced out of the party with a hamstring strain only to be recalled when he was fit again to score four tries in the quarter-final against Samoa. In the final itself, he was one of those tasked with stopping Lomu!

◀ **There have been one or two** good play-off matches – more of which anon – but England's encounter with France was a complete turkey. By common consent, not least that of the players involved, it was one of the poorest Word Cup games on record. The players, however, also reported an old-style rugby session and sing-song after the game that ended years of unhealthy enmity and real friction between the England and France camps. France won 19–9, for those of you who failed to stay awake.

▲ **President Mandela doffs his cap**
to the crowd and, you rather suspect, the
nation for their support of the Springboks.

▲ **'Francois, thank you** for what you
and your team have done for this country'
'No sir, thank *you* for what *you* have done
for this country.'

▶ **Kitch Christie** – 14 wins in 14 Tests
as coach to South Africa – celebrates with
Joel Stransky, whose extra-time drop goal
delivered victory for South Africa.

▲ **Time to honour the victors.** A few months
after the dust had settled, Mandela hosted a dinner

▲ **Art imitating life.** Morgan Freeman was looking uncannily like President Mandela by the time he had finished filming *Invictus*.

▼ **Matt Damon and Pienaar on the red carpet** before the first night of Invictus. 'I will look bigger in the film, I promise' were Damon's first words to Pienaar when they first met before the filming started.

1999

'I was weary and my calves were hurting, but everyone was in the same boat. When we got back into the action it was all really tense, but then Stephen Larkham produced a wonder drop-goal and when he did it was pure elation followed by a realisation that it still wasn't over. We had to re-focus again but eventually we managed to hold them off.'

John Eales

▼ Ready, with about five minutes to spare!
It was a race against time to complete the Millennium
Stadium in time for RWC 1999 but it was worth it.
The 74,500 capacity stadium, with its retractable roof,
immediately established itself as an iconic venue.

Previous pages: **Some people celebrate with
champagne** but the Aussies naturally marked
their 1999 triumph by dousing the Cup in the
amber nectar.

4 Wales and the Five Nations

The 1999 World Cup was a significant financial success and groundbreaking in many ways. But the decision to again allow the Five Nations, headed up by Wales as official hosts, to stage the tournament appeared flawed at times, with many matches in Scotland, France and even Ireland sometimes appearing to be peripheral to the main event. After the extraordinary success of the 1995 World Cup there was always likely to be a slight feeling of 'after the Lord Mayor's show' – how could anybody follow that? – but South Africa had also manifestly demonstrated the desirability for a single host nation, a lesson that the administrators still seemed reluctant to take on board.

In fact, the decision to award the World Cup to Wales and the other Five Nations had actually been taken in 1994, before the triumphant single country tournament in South Africa. It was notable in that, for the first time, the IRB invited nations to tender bids. The only other bid on the table was a curious hybrid intercontinental affair from Australia and Japan that stretched the imagination somewhat. The geography, logistics and finances were just too complicated and unsurprisingly didn't attract much support, so Wales and the Five Nations it was.

This was the first World Cup of the professional era and the commercial imperative was to the fore. The one big undeniable advantage of this multi-nation bid was the array of huge stadia and the large spectator base on offer and the aggregate attendance figure of 1.75 million for the tournament was impressive by any criteria. A cumulative TV audience of 3.1 billion, gross income of £70 million and net profit of £45 million were also mighty commercial figures, even if some rugby fans felt the tournament as a whole occasionally lacked a little soul.

For this tournament, RWC made a significant change in format with the number of teams competing being increased from 16 to 20 and the number of teams that qualified automatically being reduced from eight to just four. The 1995 winners South Africa, runners-up New Zealand and third-placed France were guaranteed places along with the 'host' nation, but the rest of the rugby world had to go through an admittedly none too demanding qualifying process. In total, 63 nations attempted to qualify for the 1999 tournament, meaning that in effect 75 per cent of the tournament had been

played before the first whistle in Cardiff to start the 'opening game' between Wales and the Pumas.

The increase in teams from 16 to 20, and the decision to divide them into five pools and not four, resulted in the controversial introduction of quarter-final play-offs for some teams, an instantly unpopular experiment. How it 'worked' was that after the five pool winners had been decided, the five runners-up and the best third-placed team were drawn against each other in an extra knockout round to decide the three other participants. These matches were to be played in midweek just three or four days before the quarter-finals. This is how England, Argentina and Scotland progressed and certainly the first two teams encountered serious fatigue problems when they played their quarter-finals. Coaches had complained about the system in advance and loudly repeated their criticism afterwards. The experiment was dropped thereafter.

The Welsh dragon breathes fire

The tournament started amid a deal of Welsh song and pageantry – Shirley Bassey, Tom Jones, Max Boyce, the Stereophonics, the London Welsh Male Voice Choir – at the recently completed £124 million Millennium Stadium, which had sprung up on the site of the old Cardiff Arms Park. Completing the stadium in time was a close run thing. At the official ground-testing game, a friendly against South Africa in June 1999, only 20,000 fans had been allowed into what was effectively a building site, but the contractors just squeezed home in time and the result was a magnificent 74,500 capacity stadium with a roof that could be opened and closed, depending on the weather.

The Millennium Stadium was the venue for one of the best pool games, another epic encounter between Wales and Samoa, and again the Pacific Islanders were at their best in a thrilling 38-31 win. In their own way, Samoa were a powerhouse rugby nation, an island of barely 150,000 citizens, who consistently punched way above their weight. It says much about their progress that the result was in no way a major surprise, even though Wales were much improved under Graham Henry going into the tournament.

'Frankly I hope the boys don't get over the loss in a hurry,' said Henry afterwards. 'I want them to remember how bad it feels. You develop as a team by absorbing the lessons of defeat rather than pretending it never happened. Losing can often give you a much sharper mental edge and you only need to look at the Samoans for evidence of that. Being beaten (32-16 in their previous match) by Argentina wounded them and they came out against us desperate to atone.'

Luckily for the hosts, two high-scoring wins in the opening games were enough to see them through into the quarter-finals.

Elsewhere, the pool stages were generally low key, with only sporadic moments of excellence and genuine excitement. Jonah Lomu scored an absolute corker of a try at Twickenham after England had drawn level at 16-16, to take that game out of reach of Clive Woodward's side, while Fiji were distinctly unlucky on a sweltering hot afternoon in Toulouse against France, who finally put daylight between themselves and the islanders with a late and rather controversial penalty try. At Welford Road, Tonga claimed a famous win over a disappointing Italy side with an injury-time drop goal from 50 metres by Sateki Tuipuloto.

Teamwork: A rugby team is nothing without a powerful team ethic and after the humbling 'Tour of Hell' in 1998 Clive Woodward was keen to re-establish that ethos. Martin Corry, Will Green and Mike Tindall re-enact a combat scenario with the Marines.

Getting ready for battle. England's Matt Dawson lugs a 30lb munitions box through the mud of the Exe estuary, where England held one of their pre-tournament camps with the Royal Marines.

The crowds were disappointing up in Scotland, while the fare was fairly routine over in Ireland where Australia were going quietly about their business. The 'Irish' pool was illuminated, however, by one riotous afternoon at Thomond Park, which made its long awaited debut as an international ground. The atmosphere for the game between Australia and the USA crackled from the start and claims, written large on posters as you drove in from Shannon airport, that Limerick was 'the home of the spirit of rugby' did not seem overblown as the Munster fans transformed a seemingly routine game between World Cup favourites and minnows into a wonderful festive occasion which batted on late into the night. The USA bravely responded and although eventually beaten 55-19 could at least look back and reflect that they were the only team in the entire tournament to cross the Australians' line. One of the Australian mantras going into the tournament was that they wanted to '"go nude" in every game', i.e. not concede any tries; the USA had put them straight on that point.

In the play-offs, England had to work harder than they would have wished against a Fiji side that had already shown its mettle, Scotland again demonstrated their ability to deal with Samoa's physicality, which left Ireland tackling the Pumas in the French football city of Lens in front of a sparse crowd on a chilly Wednesday night. The circumstances were not promising, but sport is perverse and a tense, enthralling encounter started to unfold between two rugged teams on the edge of elimination going toe to toe. The world-class kicking of David Humphreys and Gonzalo Quesada, who emerged as the tournament's top scorer, kept the scoreboard ticking over but eventually with less than two minutes left it was diminutive Pumas' wing Diego Albanese who struck for the game's only try and sealed victory. Back in Buenos Aires, the Stock Exchange transactions had been suspended for the final 20 minutes of the game, with the attention of many traders elsewhere.

Supernatural

A few days later the quarter-finals were upon us. On a wet day, Wales opted to leave their roof open and paid the consequences as Australia moved untroubled to a 23-9 win. Afterwards, Aussie centre Tim Horan queried that decision with a nice analogy: 'If you have a roof you should use it. It's a bit like having a Ferrari in the garage but then catching the bus.'

Scotland mounted spirited resistance at Murrayfield against New Zealand before losing 30-18, but England disappeared without trace in the second half against South Africa in Paris in the most extraordinary circumstances as Jannie de Beer, the Springboks' fourth choice fly-half just six months earlier, kicked a world record five drop goals. It appeared an ad hoc tactic. However, the very considerable rugby brain of Brendan Venter, serving a suspension after being sent off against Uruguay, had identified that England had been standing off in defence throughout the tournament and were likely to be vulnerable against the drop goal. De Beer had been practising the move much more than usual in midweek training, but five in a row and a personal tally of 34 points? That man had diamonds on the soles of his shoes.

'Some of the things that happened out there were supernatural,' mused de Beer afterwards. 'God gave us this victory and I am happy to be part of his game plan. I thank the Lord for the talent he gave me and I thank my forwards for the ball they gave me.'

The 44-21 defeat offered up an awkward moment for England's coach Clive Woodward who, during the difficult building phase when he first took over, had asked to be judged on England's performance in the World Cup. Come that moment it had been a curate's egg of a campaign but his backers at the RFU had evidently seen enough to continue their support through to 2003, one of their better decisions. The remaining quarter-final, a free-running affair in Dublin, was evenly poised with 15 minutes to go with France defending a precarious 30-26 lead over Argentina. But the travel-weary Pumas, who had scarcely had a chance to digest their historic win over Ireland, hit a physical wall and eventually went down 47-26.

Not going to script

The semi-finals were undoubtedly the crowning glory of the 1999 tournament, two matches in the space of 24 hours at Twickenham watched by 150,000 spectators. The first, Australia's 27-21 win over South Africa, was a titanic, tense arm wrestle decided in extra time when Stephen Larkham kicked one of only two drop goals in his 102-Test international career and Matthew Burke slotted the last of his eight penalties.

'It built to a great climax with us three points ahead in the dying minutes of regular time and then we fell foul of Owen Finegan's hand in the ruck,' recalls Aussie skipper John Eales.

'We knew Jannie de Beer would get the penalty from there so none of us felt "gutted", we just regrouped and started to focus immediately on extra time. I was weary and my calves were hurting, but everyone was in the same boat. When we got back into the action it was all really tense, but then Stephen Larkham produced a wonder drop-goal and when he did it was pure elation followed by a realisation that it still wasn't over. We had to re-focus again but eventually we managed to hold them off.'

The second semi-final remains a strong contender for the greatest Test match ever played, France defying logic and rugby sense to come back from a 24-10 deficit against the All Blacks to score 33 unanswered second-half points in 27 minutes en route to a truly remarkable 43-31 victory. The sight and sound of France being roared on by a largely British crowd was one to behold. Throughout the first half, New Zealand had looked nigh on irresistible and Lomu powered over for two cracking scores – the last of his World Cup record 15 tries – but after the break,

seemingly from nowhere, something suddenly flicked mentally with the French and it was 'game on'.

Firstly they nudged back through the boot of the underrated and canny Christophe Lamaison and then they let rip with tries for Lamaison, Philippe Bernat-Salles and Richard Dourthe while Jeff Wilson scored a late try for New Zealand, which offered no consolation whatsoever. At the end of the game, rather symbolically, New Zealand flanker Josh Kronfeld took off his distinctive scrum-cap and offered it to his opposite number, Olivier Magne. It was a fitting gesture from the vanquished to the victor.

So it was an Australia-France final, which wasn't what the experts had anticipated, as Eales noted on the eve of the match: 'The All Blacks were the favourites, the Springboks were defending champions and England were the great local hope. As it turned out none of those teams made the final – it was Australia against the French. That's tournament rugby, it doesn't always go to script.'

As was the case in 1987, France could not back up their semi-final heroics in the final, which was something of an anticlimax. Australia ran out 35-12 winners, almost the most routine win of their entire campaign and the most one-sided World Cup final in history. Australia were simply too good and some of the senior players, such as centre Tim Horan, had time to realise, and relish, the fact that their World Cup odyssey was drawing to a close. 'There were four of us – myself, Joe Roff, Jason Little and Daniel Herbert – still sitting in the baths smoking cigars while everybody was waiting on the bus,' he recalls. 'We just didn't want to leave because we knew that once we left the dressing room that was it.' Well, it certainly was for another four years at least and, of that quartet, Roff had one more World Cup appearance to come.

◀ **Scott Quinnell of Wales,** going through his blonde phase, skips through the tackle of Gonzalo Quesada of Argentina during the opening Rugby World Cup Pool D match at the Millennium Stadium in Cardiff, Wales.

▶ **As in previous World Cups** some of the smaller venues proved very successful. Thomond Park, the Munster citadel, whipped up a fantastic atmosphere on and off the pitch for what threatened to be a fairly routine match for champions elect Australia and minnows USA.

▲ **Rugby has a long tradition** of streakers dating back to Erica Roe in 1982 and this Aussie fan did her best to maintain that when the Aussies played Romania in Belfast.

◀ **Nobody is perfect** but Australia captain John Eales came closer than most mere mortals, hence his nickname, 'Nobody'. Here he rises high during Australia's 57-9 win over Romania at Ravenhill.

▼ **Jonah Lomu was far from comfortable** with the adulation and acclaim that followed him. More often than not he disappeared behind his dark glasses and a wall of sound. Back home he spent $100,000 rigging his Nissan Patrol car as a 'Boom Box', which recorded 167 decibels in one competition.

▼ **Australia thrived in Ireland** during the knockout stages of the 1991 World Cup, loving the ambience of Dublin, and were delighted to find themselves in the 'Irish' based pool in 1999. Lock Matt Cockbain tests a knee strain with an early morning run at the famous Portmarnock Golf Links.

◀▼ Not long after the 1995 World Cup
Jonah Lomu became seriously ill, developing a kidney disease, nephrotic syndrome, which was eventually to require dialysis and then a full kidney transplant. When he appeared at RWC1999, the condition was being controlled by strong medication but remarkably he was still in fantastic shape and effective as ever. Having emerged seemingly from nowhere to be the top try scorer in 1995, with seven tries, Lomu topped that with eight tries four years later. Against England in the pool stages, pictured here, he was as dominant as ever, scoring a game-changing try every bit as good as anything from their game four years earlier as he powered past or through Austin Healey and Jonny Wilkinson.

▲ **Before the key Australia pool game** Ireland deliberately tried to get away from it all in rural Clonakilty, famed for its cattle, black pudding, beautiful beaches and Shanley's Music Bar. Perhaps they arrived back at Lansdowne Road a little too relaxed.

◀ **Ireland flanker Trevor Brennan** retires to his corner after trading blows with Australia's Toutai Kefu. Brennan received a one-week ban for his troubles, while Kefu received a two-week sanction.

▲ **Injuries plagued Ben Tune's career** but when
fully fit and in full flight he was a mighty performer.
A youthful Brian O'Driscoll tries in vain to prevent
the Wallaby wing scoring a late try in Australia's
comfortable 23-3 win over Ireland.

▼ **Tim Horan was a teenage World Cup winner in 1991** and overcame a series of career-threatening knee injuries to claim a second winners' medal in 1999, when he was acclaimed as the player of the tournament. Sharp on the break, his defence was excellent and he always knew where the try-line was. Here he scores against Ireland.

◀ **Captain Pat Lam** always led by example for Samoa and you can feel his joy as he runs in this try against Wales in his side's 38-31 pool win at the Millennium Stadium.

▲ **Lightning doesn't strike twice, does it?**
Welsh fans believed their loss to Western Samoa in 1991 was a one-off against a less than vintage Wales team. It could never happen again. Eight years on, a much stronger and improved Wales team under coach Graham Henry met the same fate against the exuberant Islanders, losing 38-31 on this occasion.

▲ **Australia's captain for the day, Jason Little,** stops Juan Grobler on this occasion. The US Eagles centre did, however, have the satisfaction of scoring the only try against the Wallabies in the entire tournament earlier in their pool game at Thomond Park, which the Wallabies won 55-19.

▼ (*and previous page*) **Argentina's quarter-final play-off victory** was joyously celebrated on the pitch at Lens, while it caused the temporary suspension of trading at the Buenos Aires Stock Exchange while traders crowded around TV monitors to watch the closing stages of the match.

▲ **The quarter-final play-offs** experiment was short-lived, leaving the winners at an unfair disadvantage when they played the quarter-finals proper four days later, which included travelling time. The Pumas were as plucky as ever but went down 47-26 to a much improved France in their quarter-final in Dublin.

▲ ▶ **New Zealand were strong favourites to win** their semi-final against France, although the French had hinted at a return to their best form in their quarter-final against the Pumas a week earlier in Dublin. To start with, all went according to the script, with two tries from the unstoppable Jonah Lomu and the reliable boot of Andrew Mehrtens seeing New Zealand build a 24-10 lead shortly after half-time. Up in the stands, some fans were already on their mobiles planning their visits to Cardiff for a final against Australia. At which point the French begged to differ...

◀ **...First the canny Christophe Lamaison**, enjoying the best game of his career, nudged France back into serious contention with two shrewd drop goals and a brace of penalties. Then France began to build up a head of steam, Christophe Dominici (pictured) lighting the touch paper with a well-taken try and Richard Dourthe adding a second. Suddenly a packed Twickenham was echoing to the chant of 'Allez les Bleus'.

▼ **Photo finish. It looks nip and tuck** as Jeff Wilson and the old silver fox Philippe Bernat-Salles go head to head for France's third and final touchdown but it was the Frenchman who got there first. From 24-10, France had scored 33 unanswered points in 27 minutes. Jeff Wilson scored a late try for New Zealand but, to the disbelief of the rugby world France were the 43-31 winners. Many commentators still consider it the greatest World Cup game ever.

◀ **France prop Frank Tournaire** enjoys the moment with his two year old daughter

▼ **Whenever New Zealand lose** there is always an inquest, let alone after a calamitous semi-final defeat. Coach John Hart (centre) and assistant Peter Sloane try to make sense of it all.

The Final

◀ **Tim Horan was MOM in his last ever World Cup match,** spearheading Australia's 35-12 win against a France side that had nothing left after their semi-final heroics. Horan played in 14 World Cup matches in three tournaments and lost just once - against England in the 1995 quarter-final.

▲ **Seven penalties from Matt Burke** had seen Australia build a 21-0 lead over the French before Ben Tune crashed over for the first of their two tries. Replacement flanker Owen Finegan added a second before the end.

◀ **George Gregan enjoyed a cracking tournament** for the Australians, both as a scrum-half and John Eales' lieutenant. Victory was very sweet indeed.

2003

'We came very close to blowing it. After half-time every decision seemed to go against the lads and yet they still found a way of winning which is the sign of a champion team. In many ways our final play of the game summed up what we were about, going straight back from the penalty to make it 17–17 and producing the precise play that the situation demanded under extreme pressure.'

Clive Woodward England Coach

By 2003 the World Cup opening ceremony was a colourful and lavish affair.

previous pages. 22 November 2003. Jonny Wilkinson goes down the tunnel as a World Cup winner. Injuries meant he didn't pull on an England shirt again until 3 February 2007.

5

Australia

Such had been England's form and dominance under Clive Woodward in the preceding years that the 2003 World Cup was always going to be England's to lose, which can be a tricky situation as the rugby world waits for you to trip up or encounter a random bad day at the office. After underperforming at the 1999 tournament, England kicked on at the start of the new millennium with their improvement based squarely on their willingness to seek out matches at every possible opportunity against the southern hemisphere giants New Zealand, South Africa and Australia. From June 2000, when they beat South Africa in the second Test match of a short series at Bloemfontein, England embarked on an unprecedented run of 14 straight wins against the SANZAR heavyweights.

Woodward's vision

Woodward's approach was to use specialist coaches in every conceivable area of the game and to adopt a logical and coherent 'business plan' for the process of winning a World Cup. The coach had been particularly impressed with a presentation by businessman Humphrey Walters, who ran the training company MaST International. Walters talked about his experience of helping one crew of 11 yachts entered in the BT Global Challenge – an event in which identical yachts were raced by amateur crews under the guidance of a professional skipper. With none of the 11 teams having any advantage in terms of equipment, technology and manpower, Walters argued that the winning team would process 1 per cent better than any of the others. It was the basis of the 'aggregation of marginal gains' philosophy that was later also to underpin the rise and rise of British cycling under Sir Dave Brailsford.

This chimed loudly with Woodward as a basic philosophy and importantly he convinced the RFU's CEO Francis Baron that this was the right way forward. Woodward's budget was increased, enabling him to employ a succession of specialist coaches or experts – rugby-based, medical, conditioning and nutritional – to fine-tune every conceivable aspect of the process. Amid much scepticism, he even hired a South African visual performance coach, Dr Sherylle Calder, and attracted much mirth by attaching

▲ **Calm before the storm.**
England enjoy a little downtime on Cottesloe beach in Perth before the action begins.

a QC, Richard Smith, to the squad to deal with any disciplinary appeals and legal matters. It seemed excessive at the time but Woodward had the last laugh when Smith was pressed into service on England's behalf at a vital stage during the tournament.

There were a few bumps along the way with Grand Slams going begging at Wembley in 1999-2000 when England lost to Scotland at Murrayfield and 2001 when England were beaten by Ireland in Dublin, but generally the graph was upwards.Twelve months out from the World Cup, England embarked on a remarkable rampaging orgy of winning rugby. In the 2002 November internationals they beat Australia, New Zealand and South Africa before marching to a commanding Six Nations Grand Slam in the spring of 2003. On a roll, Woodward took a full-strength side 'down south' again that summer and recorded famous road wins against New Zealand and Australia before completing his preparations with a series of friendlies back home. He put out a largely Second XV against Wales in Cardiff and won 43-9, while a similar side went down by one point to France in Marseille. The following week a full-strength England blew the French away 45-14 at Twickenham. England travelled to Australia in expectation rather than hope, the onus firmly on the rest of the world to find a way of derailing them.

AUSTRALIAN ENTREPRENEURIAL SKILL

The World Cup that awaited them had been altered again after the generally agreed failure of the quarter-final play-off system in 1999. The solution was simple: instead of five pools of four teams, the competition would now consist of four pools of five teams, with the top two progressing to the quarter-finals. Much better, and that is the format that has remained ever since.

The 2003 tournament had originally been granted to Australia and New Zealand, who tendered a joint bid, but a growing indication of the strict commercial rules that now applied to Rugby World Cup came in 2002 when New Zealand had co-host status taken away from them because they had to reluctantly concede that they were unable to guarantee 'clean stadiums' for licensed World Cup sponsors. New Zealand were still contractually obliged to grant their existing domestic sponsors advertising space at all the major grounds, which went against RWC protocol.

No compromise or 'buy out' could be agreed so Australia became the sole hosts of RWC 2003. They did a superb job, taking rugby to every state save for Northern Territories, while their large ex-pat population, spread throughout the country, ensured that virtually all the games attracted large, passionate crowds. Even

when the ex-pat element was missing, Australia demonstrated typical entrepreneurial skill, not least in the non-rugby playing state of Tasmania. State capital, Launceston, was the venue for the clash of the minnows, Romania against Namibia. In the run-up to the game, media outlets encouraged locals living in odd-numbered houses to cheer for Romania, while those in even-numbered houses supported Namibia. Result? A full house. Genius.

The pool stages, ultimately, panned out very much as expected but were not without interest. Pool A provided the most drama. One of hosts Australia, Ireland or Argentina was going to miss out on the quarter-finals. That made for tight, sudden death, knockout style rugby when that trio played each other and a ruthless attempt to improve their points' difference when they met hapless Namibia and Romania. Ultimately, Ireland's rugged 16-15 win over Argentina at the Adelaide Oval cricket ground saw them qualify in second position behind Australia, although the Irish could have topped the pool if they had managed to convert pressure into points and defeat the Aussies at the Telstra Dome in Melbourne. Instead they went down 17-16 in one of the best games of the tournament.

England's Pool C hinged totally on their game against South Africa at the Subiaco Oval in Perth where, a year after an explosively bad-tempered and ill-disciplined performance from South Africa at Twickenham, further carnage and retribution was predicted. As it happened, England, with Kyran Bracken enjoying a career best performance opposite Boks' danger man Joost van der Westhuizen, enjoyed a fairly routine and untroubled 25-6 win. The only cloud on their horizon en route to the quarter-finals was a sub-par performance against the always dangerous Samoans in Melbourne. England recovered their poise sufficiently to win 35-22, but not without controversy. At one stage, with Mike Tindall receiving treatment, England managed to have 16 players on the field for 34 seconds with Dan Luger coming on without anybody going off, making one tackle in the process. It was a seemingly trivial incident, but the result could have been disastrous if the RWC organisers had decided to dock England points. In the end, Richard Smith QC managed to limit the damage to a £10,000 fine – a definite 'result' for Woodward's careful preparations.

The match had been a warning shot for England, and the Australian press were right on their case. 'Is that all you've got?' asked the *Sydney Morning Herald* mischievously, having already dubbed England's extremely experienced team 'Dad's Army' at the start of the tournament. England refused to rise to the bait and

▶ **The Australian sporting public** got right behind the smaller teams and helped make the tournament. Romania's outstanding flanker Ovidiu Tonița celebrates a try against Namibia down in Launceston, Tasmania.

◀ **711 schoolchildren combined forces** to form 'Rocky the Rugby player', who featured prominently in the opening ceremony before Australia's game against Argentina.

maintained a diplomatic silence. Their reply was always best made on the pitch.

Elsewhere, the brilliant but wayward and ill-disciplined Rupeni Caucaunibuca scored the try of the tournament for Fiji against France and another brace against Scotland that were nearly as good. Unfortunately, he missed Fiji's other matches through suspension. France looked dominant in their group, as did New Zealand, although they received a shock to the system in their final game against Wales. Resting players and making a few positional switches ahead of their already for what seemed like a guaranteed quarter-final against England, New Zealand suddenly found themselves up against a revitalised side playing exhilarating high-tempo rugby. For a while an extraordinary shock win seemed possible, until New Zealand recovered to win a remarkable game 53-37.

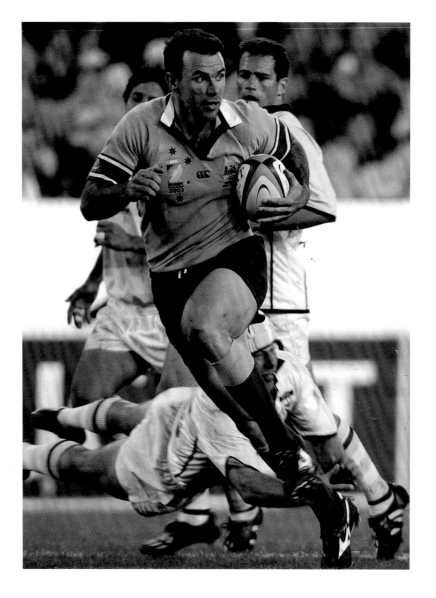

JONNY PUTS HIS BOOTS ON

Wales started their quarter-final against England where they finished off against the All Blacks. They shook the favourites to the core in the first half at the Suncorp Stadium in Brisbane. It was only when Mike Catt came on after the break that England were able to restore tactical order, and a moment of genius from Jason Robinson set up Will Greenwood for the decisive score in a 28-17 victory. New Zealand made short work of a disappointing South Africa team in Melbourne to cruise into the semi-finals with a 29-9 win. Twenty-four hours later, at the same venue, a first-half blitzkrieg from France did for Ireland, whose captain and talisman Keith Wood announced his retirement after their 43-21 defeat. In the remaining quarter-final, Scotland gave a decent account of themselves against Australia, but the hosts were too strong and moved smoothly through to the next phase with a 33-16 win.

The semi-finals saw two wildly contrasting days. Brilliant scalding sunshine on the Saturday witnessed Australia's rapturously received and surprisingly straightforward 20-9 win over great rivals New Zealand in a match notable mainly for a fine example of sportsmanship from All Blacks prop Kees Meeuws. When a scrum collapsed early in the second half, his opposite number, Ben Darwin, sensed a loud crack in his neck and started to lose all feeling from a prolapsed disc. He cried out 'neck, neck, neck'. Meeuws immediately stopped pushing in an effort to take all the pressure off his opponent. 'I was very fortunate and have Kees to thank for his prompt action, it could have got very serious,' recalls Darwin. 'I lost all feeling in my body for a couple of minutes, but thank God I soon started to get pins and needles sensations as the medical staff treated me.' Darwin had to retire from the game, but he walked unaided from the hospital a few days later. In contrast, an evening of miserable cold rain was brightened only by Jonny Wilkinson, who kicked all of England's points as they comprehensively outmuscled France 24-7.

◀ **Wing Joe Roff** impressed throughout the tournament, starting with Australia's opening game against Argentina.

▶ **England was a team of all the talents** ... but they also had the world's best goal-kicker. Jonny Wilkinson bangs over another three points.

Nobody could argue that in terms of the rugby played these two teams were worthy finalists, setting up another chapter in the book of historic rivalry between these two historic rivals who had already met on all sorts of playing fields.

The build-up was massive, not least because in addition to England's travelling support the huge ex-pat English population living in Australasia seemed determined to get their hands on every available free ticket. On the day of the game, many of them made their way up the Parramatta River in a flotilla of small boats. Judging from team colour and crowd volume, support in the stadium appeared to be split 50-50. The pressure was immense. In the first half, the rugby was free flowing. Australia opened up with a brilliantly executed try, Stephen Larkham launching a well-directed high ball towards Lote Tuqiri for the touchdown.

For reasons unknown, they never repeated that tactic. England hit back through the boot of Jonny Wilkinson and a sharply taken try by Jason Robinson. They went down the tunnel 14-5 up and it could have been more if Ben Kay had not fumbled the ball on the line just before the break.

In the second half, England began to lose the plot as they increasingly came under pressure from both the Australians and the referee Andre Watson, who began to find fault with their scrummaging. A late penalty from Elton Flatley tied the scores at 14-14 and took the game into 20 minutes' extra time. Flatley and Wilkinson swapped penalties before, going into the final minute, England implemented their 'zigzag' move from an attacking line-out and set Wilkinson up to kick a drop goal with his 'wrong' foot from 35 metres. Wilkinson had missed the previous three drop goal attempts at various stages of the match, but his confidence was undiminished ... it was time to execute. 'He drops for World Cup glory,' said Ian Robertson on the BBC, 'It's up, it's over, he's done it, Jonny Wilkinson is England's hero, yet again ... England have just won the World Cup.'

Game over? Perhaps not. Australia restarted quickly and kicked short as England tried to hurry back into position. It needed alert work from England prop Trevor Woodman to receive and recycle the ball without conceding a penalty, before Mike Catt planted the ball into the grandstand and the whistle went. The match was finally won, 20-17, the trophy was England's. At last a northern hemisphere nation had won the World Cup and 12,000 miles away, back in England, a day-long party the likes of which we haven't seen before or since got underway.

'We had to stay chilled during the build-up and let the gravitas of the match itself kick in on the day, and that's pretty much what happened,' recalls Lawrence Dallaglio, who played every minute of England's campaign in Australia. 'They got a great start, courtesy of a wonderful cross-field kick from Steve Larkham who was as good a Test 10 as I ever played against. But, no panic, and soon we ripped into them and played some very decent rugby and should have lead by more than 14-5 at half-time.

'After the break though we played as badly as I can ever remember with that group, losing the second half 9-0. We lost concentration and Andre Watson started to find fault with our dominant scrum. It could easily have gone pear-shaped, but we still had that calm inner core of belief and after going behind to that early try, we quickly got in front and hadn't been headed again. It might have appeared otherwise in the stands and back home on TV but we still felt we were dictating terms. We still felt it was our match to win. Then came the extra-time drama and the epic conclusion, but my over-riding memory of the night was the sheer pleasure of sitting in the changing room for an hour or so afterwards when we shut the door to all but VIPs and Royals and just enjoyed the moment en masse, a group of guys who possibly may never all be in the same room together again at any stage for the rest of our lives.'

The aftermath of the 2003 World Cup demonstrated clearly how big the tournament had become. More than 10,000 fans were waiting for the World Cup winning team's early morning arrival at Heathrow a couple of days later, while on 8 December, a bone-chilling freezing day from memory, police estimated that 750,000

supporters flocked to central London for the official open-top bus victory parade, which eventually came to a halt at Trafalgar Square where the party really kicked off.

'We came very close to blowing it,' reflected Woodward some time later. 'After half-time every decision seemed to go against the lads and yet they still found a way of winning, which is the sign of a champion team. In many ways our final play of the game summed up what we were about, going straight back from the penalty to level the scores at 17-17 and producing the precise play that the situation demanded under extreme pressure. That can never suddenly happen, it's the result of years and years of training, playing and learning from defeats and setbacks. They were a great bunch of players with a great captain and I was very proud and privileged to be in charge of them.'

◄ Georgian scrumhalf Merab Kvirikashvili worships at the Russian Orthodox Church in Perth on the morning of their pool game against England.

▼ Australia ran up a cricket score - 142-0 - against Namibia at the Adelaide Oval. Just as well they had the famous cricket scoreboard to cope.

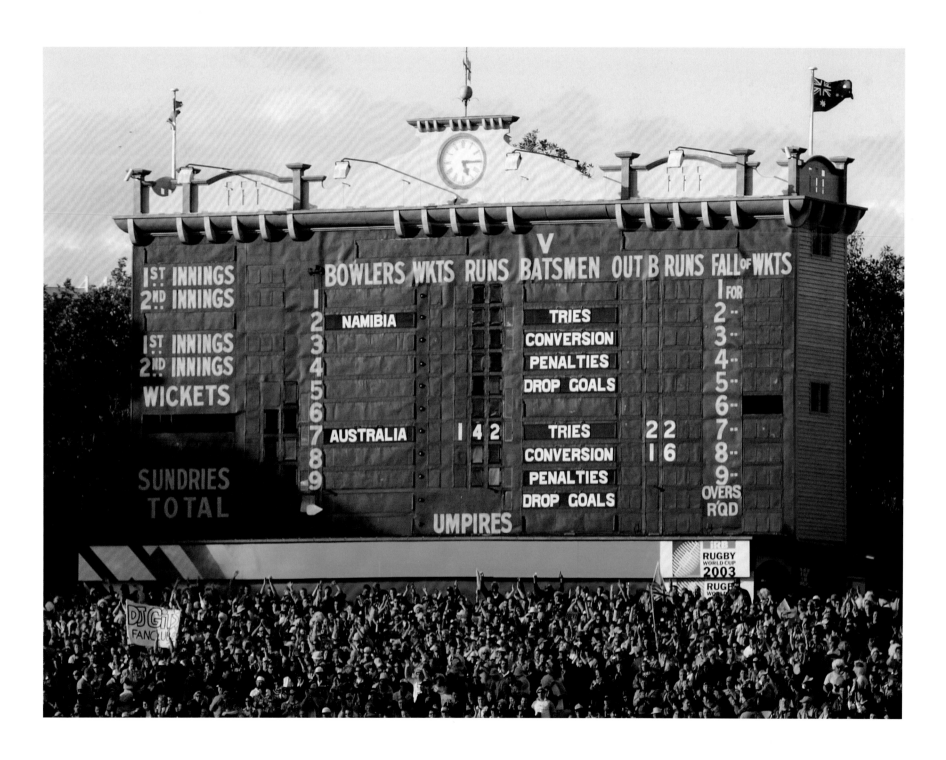

Pre-tournament and pool stages

✓ **Lote Tuqiri captained his native Fiji** in the 2000 Rugby League World Cup before switching to Union and changing his allegiance to Australia. He was a major attacking weapon for the Aussies and showed his paces early on with a hat-trick against Namibia.

◄ England was under intense scrutiny in Australia and travelled with their own security officers. Coach Clive Woodward looks to the skies during a training session at Hale School in Perth as an unidentified helicopter circles the ground, filming their session.

▲ Celtic Tiger tames Lion man! By 2003 Brian O'Driscoll was at the heart of everything good for Ireland while back in Namibia flanker Schalk van der Merwe worked as the big cat specialist at the Harnas animal sanctuary 200 miles outside Windhoek.

► The 'discovery' of RWC 2003 was Fiji's volcanic wing Rupeni Caucaunibuca, who scored sensational tries against France and Scotland although discipline was an issue and meant he missed Fiji's other two pool games.

▼ Yorke park, Launceston is usually an 'Aussie Rules' Oval but provided a splendidly scenic setting for Romania's game against Namibia in Hobart, the first full rugby international staged in Tasmania.

▶ Ireland skipper Keith Wood prepares to sidestep Australia captain George Gregan in their pool match. Ireland produced their best performance of the tournament but let a possible victory slip from their grasp, which gave them a very tough quarter-final against France.

▶ England's progress through the pools was relatively stress-free, except for a mix up in the game against Samoa, which resulted in them having 16 players on the pitch for 38 seconds. England were fined £10,000 and fitness coach Dave Reddin, who supervised the substitution, was banned from the touchline for two games. Fourth official Steve Walsh was also banned for three days after an altercation with Reddin. Crucially though England escaped being 'docked' points.

Quarter-finals

▷

▽ **England were trailing 10-3 at half-time** in their quarter-final against Wales before Mike Catt came on to change the nature of the game, giving England a second kicking option out of hand and more penetration in midfield.

▲ **Wow, that was close.**
Prince Harry and Jane Woodward, wife of England coach Clive Woodward, feeling the strain as England - outscored three tries to one - quarry out a 26-17 quarter-final win over Wales.

▶ **Lawrence Dallaglio played every single minute** of England's seven games at the World Cup. And occasionally the strain showed!

▲ **World Cups always signal the end** for some big name players. Keith Wood, embracing with long-term opponent and good friend Fabien Galthié, retired straight after the quarter-final defeat against France. Galthié himself retired from Test rugby after France's 3rd-4th play-off defeat to New Zealand.

▶ **New Zealand centre Aaron Major** collides with Victor Matfield, which generally speaking is not a good idea. Mauger survived though and New Zealand were impressive 29-9 winners in their quarter-final in Melbourne.

Semi-finals

▶ **Christophe Dominici was one of the heroes in the 1999 semi-final** against New Zealand but this trip on Jason Robinson in the 2003 semi-final earned him a yellow card. It also injured his knee and he later required surgery.

▼ **Thumbs up** and see you back here in a week's time. Lote Tuqiri acknowledges the home crowd after their satisfying semi-final win over old rivals New Zealand.

▲ **Imanol Harinordoquy** had emerged as a go-to player for France but Lawrence Dallaglio was on his case all evening.

The Final

Australia opened the scoring when Stephen Larkham hoisted an inch-perfect crossfield kick to the towering Lote Tuqiri who was marked by the diminutive Jason Robinson. Curiously it was the only time in the game Australia used such a tactic.

Jason Robinson was England's X-factor. When they needed a moment of inspiration they turned to the former Wigan and Great Britain Rugby League star. Against Wales he jinked past four or five defenders to create a simple try for Will Greenwood, while in the final he left Chris Latham for dead to score for England after Australia's early try.

◀ **To borrow from Ian Robertson**, doing the commentary for BBC Radio Five: 'And it's coming back for Jonny Wilkinson ... he drops for World Cup glory ... it's up ... its over. Jonny Wilkinson is England's hero yet again and there's no time for Australia to come back.' Actually, there was just time for Australia to quickly restart but prop Trevor Woodman was aware of the threat and fielded the ball for Mike Catt to kick deep into the crowd. If the scores had been level after extra time, a penalty kicking competition would have ensued.

▲ **The moment of glory.** Will Greenwood starts the celebrations but Jonny Wilkinson still looks in a state of shock.

◀ **Job done.** Clive Woodward had endured some tough times early in his England coaching career but once the snowball started rolling there was no stopping his side. In 2003 they won the Six Nations Grand Slam, climbed to world number one in the IRB rankings and beat New Zealand and Australia in a quick-fire summer tour. After that, there really was only one other mountain to climb.

Australia had proved to be a brilliant host of RWC 2003 but losing to the old enemy was almost too much to take, both for the media and the fans.

Herald Sun
Sunday

NOVEMBER 23, 2003
www.sundaysun.com.au
$1.50 Inc GST

SO CLOSE

A shattered Jeremy Paul slumps to the turf as jubilant England players celebrate a hard-fought Rugby World Cup triumph. The Wallabies went within a whisker of snatching back-to-back Cups, but Jonny Wilkinson snuffed out a spirited Wallabies revival by landing 15 of England's 20 points. Reports Pages 4-5 and Sport liftout.

▲ An astonishing number of England fans besieged Sydney for the final. An estimated 35,000 somehow obtained tickets for the match itself but the remainder wore the colours at various big screen venues around the city. The steps of the Opera House proved a favourite spot to sing out their joy.

◀ **The true impact of England's World Cup win** was probably best seen back home. Police estimate that 750,000 fans packed central London for the victory parade on 8 December, which was followed by a reception at No 10 Downing Street.

▲ **Can it really be ten years ago?** Jonny Wilkinson joined a parade of England's World Cup winners at Twickenham before England's autumn international against Australia in November 2013.

2007

'This is much bigger than South African rugby. To see our State President on the shoulders of one of our players with the Webb Ellis trophy in his hands, there is no bigger statement in our country than that. We need as a nation to understand how big this is... there is a lot we can draw from this little trophy.'

Jake White South Africa Coach

South Africa may have won RWC 2007 but for many the tournament will be remembered as Argentina's 'coming out' party - the occasion when the Pumas announced themselves as a major rugby nation that badly needed to be granted entry into the game's elite.

6 France

It might have taken until 2007 for France to stage the Rugby World Cup but in truth France had hosted the rugby world for generations, both in the old French championship and the reconstituted T14, a league that often seemed to be the melting pot of the global game. The resulting tournament in France in 2007 was, for the most part, a unique ambience with players and fans alike relishing the setting. Smarting from their poor showing four years earlier, South Africa looked like a class above right from the off, and in Bryan Habana – a man who could outrun a cheetah, according to one advertisement, and a predatory try scorer who gave them a different dimension when they needed it most – they possessed the player of the tournament. To nobody's surprise it was the Boks who eventually claimed their second World Cup. But this was a compelling and entertaining tournament during which there was very much a feeling of rugby 'coming home'. National teams, such as Argentina, Georgia, Romania and Italy, simply wouldn't exist in the form that we know them without the teeming breeding ground that is the French championship, while France had also provided the opportunity for Pacific Island players to earn a living playing rugby. For many in those teams, France was the 'mother country' where they had been welcomed with open arms, settling among friends and putting down roots.

Six Nations teams and fans were, of course, well acquainted with French rugby and knew many of the venues from Heineken Cup weekends. Many of the matches had French-style late kick-offs, at 9 p.m., which added to an already distinctive and intimate atmosphere, a feeling of rugby being *en fête*. A bloody good time was had by just about everybody.

▲ Juan Martin Hernández operated under the nickname of El Magico (the Magician) and was at the peak of his powers for Argentina at RWC 2007.

Ireland and England struggle

Well, there were one or two exceptions. England struggled initially before staging a remarkable comeback to join the party and mount a credible defence of their title, but Ireland, mystifyingly, never got their act together and tumbled out of the tournament before the knockout stages. Everything had seemed perfectly set up for the Irish, who had risen to number three in the IRB world rankings following wins over South Africa and Australia in November 2006 and had then finished as runners-up in the 2007 Six Nations,

a championship they really should have won with a Grand Slam.

In the build-up, Ronan O'Gara, nothing if not a realist on the pitch, even offered the opinion that Ireland should be thinking of winning the World Cup, but come the tournament they struggled horribly against outsiders Namibia and Georgia in Bordeaux and suffered comprehensive defeats against France and old rivals Argentina at the Stade de France. Various theories were offered as to their underperformance: too much training, too little playing, lack of match fitness, arriving in France undercooked, disharmony in the camp. Who knows? But it was an ignominious exit, to say the least, and the beginning of the end for coach Eddie O'Sullivan, who had done so much to secure a place on top table for Irish rugby.

Initially, England were scarcely better with an unimpressive 28-10 win in their opening game against USA at Lens, followed by a depressing 36-0 thumping against South Africa at the Stade de France. Something seemed very wrong, but the reappearance of Jonny Wilkinson steadied the ship next time out against a less than vintage Samoa team. The forwards too put on a better show in a 44-22 win. England duly clinched their quarter-final spot with a 36-20 victory over Tonga at a soaking wet Parc des Princes on a night when simply winning was the name of the game.

Elsewhere, Australia, England's quarter-final opponents, had looked very solid in topping Pool B with a 32-10 win over Wales at the Millennium Stadium as their signature performance. Wales didn't lack firepower, but leaked way too many tries. This proved costly in their final pool game when they lost 38-34 in a thrilling encounter against Fiji in Nantes, which featured sensational attacking skills with Wales scoring five tries to Fiji's four – although neither of the two defence coaches will have been overly delighted. Wales were out and their coach Gareth Jenkins was soon to depart, to be replaced by Warren Gatland. Wales' captain Gareth Thomas was presented with a special commemorative cap to mark his 100th international appearance for Wales after the match but as he ruefully commented, 'I would happily give that cap back today for a win, that's all I wanted.'

In Pool C New Zealand, on a mission it would seem, accumulated 309 points in their four games, which was highly impressive, but you did wonder if the lack of a serious hit-out could possibly unhinge them come the quarter-finals. In Pool D, with Ireland faltering, it was Argentina and France who moved through with the unbeaten Pumas finally beginning to fulfil their potential and make their mark on the world scene. Half of the Argentinian squad lived and played in France; six of their starting pack were regulars in the French championship. The Pumas' greatest ever generation of players, including full-back Ignacio Corleto, utility back Felipe Contepomi, captain and scrum-half Gus Pichot, hooker Mario Ledesma, prop Rodrigo Roncero, lock Patricio Albacete and No. 8 Gonzalo Longo, were seasoned international performers by this stage of their careers and were determined to seize the chance of finally achieving something special together. Meanwhile, new blood had arrived in the form of fly-half Juan Martin Hernández – *El Magico* as he was dubbed – and outstanding back-row prospect Juan Martin Fernández Lobbe; this was their moment too. Argentina played with a hunger and vibrancy that lit up the tournament.

THE TOURNAMENT OPENS UP

The quarter-finals were a fascinating mix. They began in Marseille when an Andrew-Sheridan-inspired England pack scrummaged Australia into oblivion to deliver an unexpected 12-10 victory for Phil Vickery's team, while in Cardiff that night there was even more drama as pre-tournament favourites New Zealand squandered a 13-3 lead and went down 20-18 to France, both sides scoring two tries apiece. The drama centred on the New Zealand fly-halves Dan Carter and his replacement Nick Evans, who both went off injured in the second half. This left New Zealand indecisive and occasionally rudderless in the final moments when a previously unthinkable defeat started to become a reality. At 20-18 down with New Zealand pressing hard, the situation cried out for somebody to take on the responsibility and pop over a drop goal. It was a Jonny Wilkinson moment but nobody stepped forward for New Zealand, who kept battering away with no apparent game plan. Eventually, the final whistle blew and a stunned All Blacks party were on their way home. But the French effort had been titanic. Nothing exemplifies that more than the official match stats, and a subsequent examination of the 'match tape', which show that France flanker Thierry Dusautoir made an incredible 38 tackles during the game, surely a 'world's best' performance at this level.

Many claimed it was the biggest wake-up call in New Zealand's rugby history, but out of the humiliation and disappointment was forged a new resolve and pragmatism. As New Zealand's captain Richie McCaw said afterwards: 'If we knew the answers we would have sorted it out. We will be thinking about it for a long time.'

◀ **Life's a beach.** Fiji enjoyed the early autumn sun on their backs and the laid-back ambience of France and produced probably their best World Cup showing yet.

▶ **Head for the hills.** France spent a long period of the summer of 2007 in camp at Val d'Isère running up and down the local peaks. Veterans Raphael Ibanez, Serge Betsen and Yannick Jauzion lead from the front.

With New Zealand gone the tournament was wide open and the following day South Africa, not without alarm, overcame the spirited Fijians in the sunshine of Marseille with the Islanders again hinting at what a force they could become internationally given the right environment and encouragement. Fijian passion is never in doubt but their culture is very different, as skipper Mosese Rauluni indicated afterwards: 'In one of the boy's villages, they have to carry the one TV to the top of the mountain just to get some reception so they can watch the games. Those hard-core fans are the ones we play for.' Argentina, with definite hints of nerves and altitude sickness as they approached the summit of the game, managed to scrape through 19-13 at the Stade de France against a Scotland team that only started to believe in itself and really play in the final quarter.

'There's a lot we can draw from this little cup'

As the semi-finals drew near, England, apparently down and out after their 36-0 defeat to South Africa in the pool match, appeared to be on a roll. An odd campaign seemed odder still in the closing weeks when Kenny Rogers' song *The Gambler* was adopted as England's team song after prop Matt Stevens, a very decent musician and singer, started strumming it in the back of the team bus one day. Suddenly Rogers, the American Country and Western legend, was sending video messages to the team, the song was back in the charts and England fans were wearing facemasks with little white beards and giving rousing renditions of the chorus to whoever would listen. These things have a life of their own and those fans were certainly *en fête* in Paris when the time came for the massive floodlit semi-final against France, reassuringly familiar World Cup foes who held no fears for England. It was tight and tense but generally England were in the ascendency even though it did need a superb last ditch tapped tackle from Joe Worsley to prevent Vincent Clerc from scoring and a Jonny Wilkinson drop goal to complete the 14-9 win. Argentina, meanwhile, finally met their match and were outmuscled by a mighty Springbok pack. Even though the 37-13 scoreline was a tad harsh, the Pumas were well beaten by the competition's standout team.

Usually the third place play-off game in any tournament is, shall we say, low key and forgettable, but in France it transcended all the usual apathy and was arguably the match of the tournament.

Hosts France were looking to finish on a high in front of their own fans and avenge their pool defeat against Argentina, while the Pumas, realising that in many ways this was the end of an era, were determined to underscore the impact they had made on the world scene.

What followed was undoubtedly Argentina's finest ever moment on a rugby field – a ruthless demolition of France, which contained brutal physicality and supreme handling skills in equal measure. They outscored France by five tries to one with a stunning display en route to a 34-10 win at the Parc des Princes, a stadium that always revels in and indeed promotes such high-octane encounters. Afterwards coach Marcello Loffreda signed off emotionally, 'Today, Argentina played an incredible game, from a technical point of view every aspect was spot on. I am so proud and grateful to all of them for the eight years we have spent together and especially to our captain Gus Pichot who has allowed

▲ **Boys, what's happening?**
Ireland arrived in France as the number three ranked team in the world but looked lethargic and short of match fitness from the start.

▶ **The French Federation**
attracted a deal of criticism by opting for so many fooball stadia ... but the Marseille Velodrome was a stunning setting.

me to share such a spectacular journey with him.'

In contrast, the final itself was a bit of a letdown. South Africa's mighty pack imposed a stranglehold for much of the game without ever quite giving the Boks the platform to cut loose through their dangerous backs, especially out wide in the shape of Bryan Habana. South Africa were good value for their 15-6 win, however – four penalties from Percy Montgomery and one from Fran Steyn played two from Wilkinson – though it was England who came closest to scoring a try. Mark Cueto will go to his grave believing he scored in the left corner two minutes into the second half when he dobbed down under extreme pressure. Referee Alain Rolland asked the question, 'Is there any reason not to award the try?' and the TMO answered in the affirmative, he believed Cueto's left foot was in touch when he touched down. Others thought his foot was in the air at that precise moment, which would have made the score legitimate. It was an extraordinarily close call at an important

stage of the game, but sport is full of those and it was Boks captain John Smit who eventually lifted the Webb Ellis trophy, although he was soon usurped in his trophy-carrying duties by his nation's president, Thabo Mbeki.

'This is much bigger than South African rugby,' mused victorious coach Jake White afterwards. 'To see our state president on the shoulders of one of our players with the Webb Ellis trophy in his hands, there is no bigger statement in our country than that. We need as a nation to understand how big this is … there is a lot we can draw from this little cup.' Absolutely, although in the ever-volatile world of South African rugby it is interesting to note that White, who was to be voted the IRB coach of the year in 2007, was soon seeking alternative employment. Following the World Cup he wanted time to consider his position, but the SARU were not willing to grant that and, World Cup winner or not, White was on his way. It was a downbeat end to a great career.

▲ **Juan Manuel Leguizamón** dives
in for a try against Namibia in Marseille.
The big flanker came of age for
Argentina in France.

▲ **By 2007 Gus Pichot was the captain**, spiritual leader, spokesman, translator for Argentina - as well as still being their linchpin at scrum-half. His time on the pitch was running out and he was determined to leave on a high.

▶ **Wow! Takudzwa Ngwenya** 'smokes' Bryan Habana in a memorable one-on-one between the two fastest wings at the tournament, in fact two of the quickest wins in rugby history. The Springboks won 60-19 but the glory on this occasion went to Ngwenya.

Quarter-finals

▲ You don't frighten me! Confronting the haka is difficult and often comes down to personal choice on the night. Christophe Dominici chose a dismissive look of contempt as New Zealand lock Ali Williams advanced with murderous intent.

▲ **2007 might have been the 'French' World Cup** but France's finest moment came at the Millennium Stadium in Cardiff when New Zealand, after strolling through their pool stage, found themselves badly undercooked. Vincent Clerc evades the clutches of Brendon Leonard.

▲ **With Dan Carter controlling the game at fly-half,** New Zealand were leading 13-3 at half-time but it all started going wrong after the break. Thierry Dusautoir scored a try, then Carter limped off with a calf injury while his replacement Nick Evans was also injured later in the game.

▶ **New Zealand full-back Leon MacDonald** cannot believe what has happened ... but in the time-honoured fashion shakes hands with France prop Pieter de Villiers.

◀ **Flanker Thierry Dusautoir** made an extraordinary 38 tackles against New Zealand! Dusautoir, born in the Ivory Coast, was only called into France's World Cup squad at the last minute because of injuries.

▶ **Coach Graham Henry stares blankly into space**, Captain Richie McCaw is lost in his own thoughts. Many in the media and back home in New Zealand pointed the finger unfairly at referee Wayne Barnes but within the New Zealand camp they knew the fault lay at their own door. To a man they vowed to do better in 2011.

▲ **The tour groups from Australia** enjoyed the scorching sun in Marseilles ... but you can sense the tension as their side begin to struggle up front.

▶ **Six England defenders** gang up on Australia's captain Stirling Mortlock.

◀ **As ever a fit again Jonny – and his goal kicking – was key** as England gradually got their act together after a humiliating 36-0 defeat to South Africa in one of their pool games.

▼ **England, unashamedly, decided to make** their quarter-final an arm-wrestle up front and a test of scrummaging power. Which made props Andrew Sheridan, of England, and Australia's Matt Dunning two of the most important players on the field. Ultimately it was Sheridan's finest hour.

▶ **Bakkies Botha rises high** for a classic line-out take against Fiji. At times, South Africa found themselves dragged into an exhilarating but high-risk handling game against the Fijians but they always had their world-class set piece to call on when needed.

▲ **They shall not pass.** Fiji were far from flattered by the 37-20 score line against South Africa in Marseille, giving the Boks the fright of their lives for much of the game. Fiji replacement Gabiriele Lovobalavu makes a last ditch tackle to prevent Boks speedster JP Pietersen breaking clear.

▶ **There was no shortage of classy wings at RWC 2007** and Fiji's Vilimoni Delasau - seen scoring here against South Africa - was yet another of the quick men who stood out.

▼ **Fiji's full-back Norman Ligairi** heads for the open spaces but Boks centre Jaque Fourie, who enjoyed a fine tournament, is alert to the danger and closes him down.

Semi-finals

▽ Joe Worsley made a big impact up front for England when he came on in the second half against France and his tapped tackle on Vincent Clerc saved an almost certain try at an important stage of the game.

▶ **Goal kicking** is sometimes all about slide rules and angles and somehow you just know Jonny Wilkinson has judged this difficult kick perfectly.

▲ **England fans gathered en masse** around the cafes and restaurants near the Gare du Nord after their semi-final win over France. First came a very late dinner and most were still there for breakfast as well.

▲ 3rd-4th play-off matches can be a damp squib but Argentina made their thunderous 34-10 win over France into a gala occasion at the Parc des Princes. In fact, it was arguably the match of the tournament and serious talks started soon after as to how they could be incorporated into either the Tri-Nations or Six Nations. Eventually they went the southern hemisphere route.

▶ Roll up, roll up. If you have £3,459.00 handy a World Cup Final ticket can be yours, no questions asked. England's unexpected march to the final caught many by surprise and come the day there was a premium pay if you insisted on being there in person.

The IRB Rugby World Cup Tickets Block: H11 Row: 59	2 tickets	£1950.00 per ticket	buy
The IRB Rugby World Cup Tickets Block: G Row: 4	2 tickets	£1950.00 per ticket	buy
The IRB Rugby World Cup Tickets Block: H Row: 6	2 tickets	£1950.00 per ticket	buy
The IRB Rugby World Cup Tickets Block: WEST BASSE R14 - BLUE CAT Row: 7	1 ticket available	£2000.00 per ticket	buy
The IRB Rugby World Cup Tickets Block: Category 1 Row: East / West	up to 8 tickets	£2450.00 per ticket	buy
The IRB Rugby World Cup Tickets Block: Cat ! Row: East Haute	up to 6 tickets	£2795.00 per ticket	buy
The IRB Rugby World Cup Tickets Block: Category 1 Row: East Haute	up to 2 tickets	£3459.00 per ticket	buy

The
Final

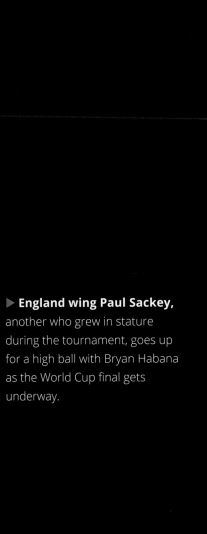

▶ **England wing Paul Sackey,**
another who grew in stature
during the tournament, goes up
for a high ball with Bryan Habana
as the World Cup final gets
underway.

▶ South Africa generally exerted an iron grip on a cagey final but the one moment England threatened to break through was early in the second half when Mark Cueto evaded the clutches of Danie Rossouw to apparently score in the corner. Referee Alain Rolland referred the TMO and it was touch and go whether Cueto's left foot was just grazing the touchline when he actually touched down. The try was disallowed, although the debate continues.

◀ South Africa knew that they had to stay disciplined and deny Jonny Wilkinson the opportunity to 'run' the game and build an England score through his goal-kicking. They succeeded on both counts.

▶ England's Toby Flood was perhaps lucky not to receive a yellow card when he pushed Percy Montgomery off the ball in the goal area. The Boks' full-back, who was the tournament's leading points scorer with 105, was sent flying into the TV cameras.

Previous pages: **The match is won and lost** and the rugby world prepares to acclaim South Africa as the 2007 world champions.

◄ **South Africa World Cup wins** tend to be political as well as sporting events. President Thabo Mbeki lost no time in parading the Cup at the Stade de France after the Springboks' 15-6 triumph.

▲ **This is for you, Mr Mandela.** The former President had maintained his close personal support for the Springboks and South Africa captain John Smit headed straight from Johannesburg airport to Mandela's home in Houghton with the Cup when the Boks arrived back in South Africa.

2011

'The RWC 2011 organisers first had to deal with the huge psychological impact of the earthquake and the inevitable worries about whether it was safe to proceed with the competition at all. Having decided it was they were then faced with the logistical nightmare of relocating those seven games with Auckland, Dunedin and Wellington largely taking up the slack. Not the least of the achievements of the 2011 World Cup is that Plan B worked faultlessly.'

New Zealand

The return of the Rugby World Cup to New Zealand 24 years after the original groundbreaking competition was laced with poignancy and nostalgia as many, mentally at least, revisited the 1987 tournament and compared it with the modern day. In terms of global reach, TV and media coverage, and the degree of professionalism of almost all those involved on and off the pitch, there was no comparison – and yet the great success of 2011 was that the New Zealand organisers still managed a significant nod to the old days in emphasising its grass-roots traditions. New Zealand is not a nation of super-stadia and even Eden Park needed temporary stands installed to bring it up to the minimum 60,000 capacity the IRB had decreed necessary for a World Cup final. But rather than bemoan its lack of world-class facilities, the NZRU chose instead to make a virtue of it, taking the World Cup out to 13 venues across the land, which was three or four more than the IRB would have ideally liked. New Zealand's big advertising mantra for the bid was 'New Zealand, a stadium of four million people' and in deference to that they wanted to stage matches in Invercargill and Whangarai, Nelson, Napier and Palmerston North, as well as the better-known venues such as Wellington, Dunedin, Hamilton and Auckland.

Double disaster

▲ **An estimated 90,000** overseas fans made it to New Zealand at some stage of the tournament, with the safe environment on offer encouraging thousands of young backpackers as well as the big tour parties.

Conspicuously missing from that list, of course, was Christchurch, which vies with Auckland as the rugby capital of a rugby-daft nation, but suffered catastrophically due to the earthquake that affected the city and surrounding areas on 22 February 2011. The events of that day resulted in nearly 200 deaths and the wide-scale destruction of major buildings and infrastructure – the ongoing rebuilding process will cost an estimated 40 billion.

Seven matches – five pool games and two quarter-finals – had been scheduled for the city's Lancaster Park, historically one of rugby's iconic grounds. Renamed Jade Stadium, it had just completed a multi-million pound upgrade when the earthquake struck with devastating effect. Huge cracks appeared in the main stands, while the pitch surface had become corrugated, rutted and totally

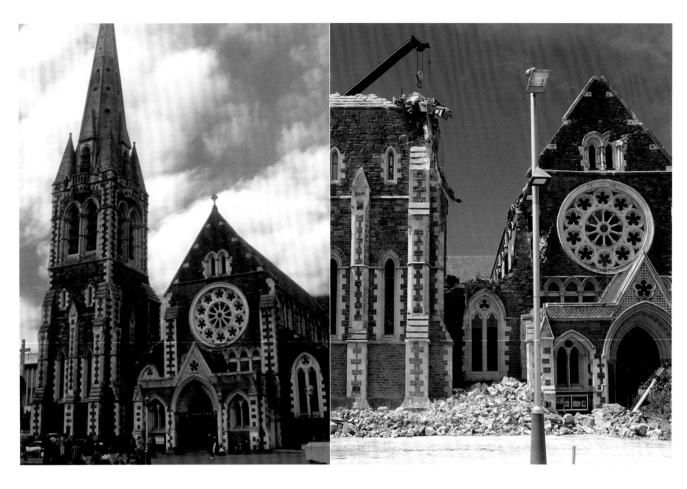

◄ **RWC 2011 was plunged into jeopardy on 22 February 2011** when an earthquake hit Christchurch and surrounds, resulting in the death of 181 people and causing massive damage to the infrastructure of the city. For many years the Anglican cathedral had been a well-known city centre landmark with its famous 6m stained-glass rose windows but, as these pictures show, it suffered grievously.

unplayable. The future of the stadium is still undecided, but in any event it seems unlikely that rugby will ever be played there again.

The RWC 2011 organisers first had to deal with the huge psychological impact of the earthquake and the inevitable worries about whether it was safe to proceed with the competition at all. Having decided it was, they were then faced with the logistical nightmare of relocating those seven games with Auckland, Dunedin and Wellington largely taking up the slack. Not the least of the achievements of the 2011 World Cup is that Plan B worked faultlessly and you would never have guessed at the blood, sweat and tears that had been shed to make the late switch.

As the start of the tournament approached, emotions were running high. As well as the earthquake, New Zealanders were also coping with the Pike River Mine disaster. On 19 November 2010, 29 miners and contractors were declared missing when the coalmine in which they were working suffered a series of methane gas explosions. Four explosions occurred over nine tense days until the authorities declared that there were no survivors. The disaster had hit the national consciousness hard.

HAKAS SET THE TONE

It could be said that the arrival of the tournament provided some welcome relief. The All Blacks were very mindful that they hadn't won a World Cup since 1987 and, apart from the 1995 tournament in South Africa, had generally underperformed since then despite their perennial status as the world's top-ranked team. It was time to settle that score and prove they were no chokers.

But what really set the tone of the 2011 World Cup were the approximately 130,000 overseas fans that visited the island, which was nearly three times more than the organisers had anticipated, and the rapturous home support the three Pacific Islands garnered from New Zealand's polyglot society. Rarely have so many hakas been done with such conviction and to such tumultuous applause.

For the second consecutive tournament, however, Samoa did not quite hit the heights, although they were in a brutal pool alongside South Africa and a resurgent Wales. Fiji, in the same pool as Samoa, also disappointed, but Tonga rose to the occasion and, roared on by their supporters, gave a more than credible performance in the opening game against New Zealand. They later claimed the most famous win in their history with a 19-14 triumph over France. Finishing third in Pool A saved them the inconvenience of having to qualify for the 2015 World Cup.

New Zealand, as usual, cruised through to the quarter-finals and it was the French who joined the All Blacks in progressing from Pool A, despite defeats against the Kiwis and that sensational loss to Tonga. Indeed, France became the only team ever to reach the knockout stages after two defeats. There were rumours of dissent in the French ranks with an unofficial senior players' cabal in dispute with their sometimes erratic and argumentative coach Marc Lièvremont, who apparently encountered resistance on account of his increasingly disciplinarian regime. As anybody who has reported on the subject over any period of time will confirm, such stories are commonplace in French rugby. Arguments accompanied by loud and passionate gesticulations are part of most French teams, successful or otherwise, but the vibes coming from the French camp certainly made for much intrigue and speculation.

Wales, meanwhile, had arrived in New Zealand full of youthful energy, vigour and harmony. They could/should have beaten South Africa in their opening game in Pool D, but they went down by one point after an entertaining contest. A huge talking point was a towering first-half penalty from James Hook, which, from the stands at the 'Cake Tin' in Wellington and on TV, appeared to go over. Officialdom deemed otherwise, and Wales had to take defeat on the chin. They did that in impressive fashion, as they amassed a pile of points against Namibia and Fiji, while their much-improved fitness allowed their natural skills to flourish in a 17-10 win against Samoa in Hamilton.

That win over the Samoans heralded a quarter-final with Ireland, who had possibly been the most impressive team from the Six Nations. Their Pool C win over Australia at Eden Park had really shaken up the competition and, given the makeup of the draw, virtually ensured the fourth consecutive north v south confrontation in the final. The key to Ireland's famous victory was a dominant display by their pack, particularly Sean O'Brien. The pack had perfected the choke tackle in which the player in possession of the ball is held up and prevented from going to ground, thereby ensuring a turnover decision. It wasn't the sole reason Ireland won, the rest of their game was also functioning well, but it proved a mighty weapon in their armoury.

▶ **England were originally going to be based in Christchurch** but there was no chance of the city being able to host any of the seven games planned there following the earthquake. The AMI Stadium itself was badly damaged with huge cracks appearing in the concrete stands and the field itself suffering potholes and rippling as molten lava beneath cooled down and solidified.

ENGLAND LOWER THE TONE

For column inches and controversy, nothing could compare with England, whose unbeaten topping of Pool B almost went unremarked amid the media furore caused by the squad's big night out in Queenstown the day after their opening win 13-9 against Argentina. Drink was taken in considerable quantities as the England players frequented a bar where dwarf-throwing was one of the attractions. Then later, in a nightclub bar, skipper Mike Tindall was pictured allegedly flirting with a 'gorgeous blonde' woman who was not his wife of three months, Zara Phillips. It was the Royal connection that unleashed the hounds of hell on to Tindall, and England's attempt to straight-bat the incident only inflamed the situation as the story dominated the headlines for days.

Thereafter, the conduct of every England player in the World Cup party was minutely examined. On the day after England were knocked out of the competition following their 19-12 quarter-final defeat against France – a scorching Sunday afternoon with Auckland harbour at its shimmering best – young centre Manu Tuilagi found himself in hot water for diving off a small harbour ferry to cool down with a swim. When the team returned to the UK there were no less than three inquiries into England's failings on and off the field, a process that coincided with coach/manager Martin Johnson's resignation. One way or another, it wasn't England's finest moment.

Of the other quarter-finals, the Celtic clash between Wales and Ireland was the pick of the bunch. In a thrilling first half, Wales kept the Irish at bay through their voracious appetite for defence and tackling. With the score at 10-10 early in the second half, they engaged a higher gear altogether and disappeared into the distance, with tries from Mike Phillips and Jonathan Davies heralding a 22-10 triumph. It was a hugely impressive performance, Wales' best ever at any World Cup. Argentina were competitive with the All Blacks for an hour before slipping to a 32-10 defeat, while in the other game Australia defied logic with a heroic defensive display led by open-side flanker Michael Hooper, to sneak a remarkable 11-9 win over South Africa.

THE X-FACTOR

So the battle-lines for the semi-finals were drawn: an all-European clash between resurgent Wales and the rebellious French, and the trans-Tasman clash between Australia and New Zealand, a match that many in that part of the world had hoped for as the final.

As well as attracting a full house to Eden Park, the Welsh game also saw the gates of the Millennium Stadium flung open back in Cardiff where another 60,000 fans, munching their breakfast butties and sipping their breakfast-time pints, watched together on the biggest of big screens. The match could scarcely have started more dramatically. After 10 minutes Wales' talismanic prop Adam Jones went off with an ankle injury. Nine minutes later, skipper Sam Warburton was controversially red-carded for a tip tackle on France's Vincent Clerc.

◀ **Training in Queenstown was no great chore.** England's Tom Palmer seems to be plucking the ball off a mountaintop as England go through a line-out routine.

▶ **There might be a more scenic rugby ground** than New Plymouth but I can't think of it. Mount Taranaki (8,261 feet) is an active volcano which, according to the experts, is due to 'blow' again any time in the next 50 years. Down below, Wales and Namibia prepare for battle.

It was a tough call by referee Alain Rolland, doubly so given the emotion and importance of the occasion, but the Irish official's decision to send him off was entirely correct as Warburton, with much dignity, admitted soon afterwards. Such driving, lifting tackles had been a grey area for a while in a game not wishing to distil legitimate aggression. However, the need to return the opposition player safely to ground is and always will be paramount. On this occasion, Warburton seemed to lose control of Clerc in the last phase of the tackle as the French wing dropped to earth.

With their captain in tears on the touchline, Wales recovered supremely well and, despite playing 61 minutes of the game short-handed, could well have won the match. As it was, they were pressing hard at the end before they went down 9-8. Only a team boasting their level of fitness could have made light of such a handicap. In many ways, it was one of their finest moments as well as their most disappointing.

The second semi-final, a 20-6 New Zealand win over Australia, was routine in comparison. The main talking point continued to be the soap opera surrounding the fly-half spot, which had plagued New Zealand through the later stages of the tournament. Dan Carter, one of the finest the game has ever seen, had sparkled against Tonga and France but then ripped his groin muscles during his daily goal-kicking practice before the Canada game. Tournament over, next stop the operating table for career-saving surgery. This was a serious blow to their plans, so a phone call went out to young Aaron Cruden, who by his own admission had been enjoying a few beers and skateboarding during the Carter drama. Colin Slade started in the quarter-final against Argentina and did well, but close to half-time he also suffered a groin injury and young Cruden was on. 'AC is the new DC', as one hurriedly printed T-shirt read.

With Slade now also out, manager Graham Henry again reached for his phone to summon another fly-half, this time Stephen Donald. 'I was down the Waikto River whitebaiting,' recalled Donald. 'I think Ted [Graham Henry's nickname] had missed me a couple of times and then I finally picked up a call from Mils Muliaina who said, "start answering your phone you idiot." So I got the message very soon afterwards.' Donald made his way to Auckland in haste and found himself on the bench for the final.

Before kick-off, it was unusually tense. Back in 1994, France had been the last team to beat New Zealand at Eden Park. France, even the apparently mutinous rabble gathered in New Zealand, were one of the few rugby nations New Zealand feared. The French sometimes bring an X-factor to proceedings that cannot be anticipated and countered, even by the always meticulous and knowing New Zealand coaching staff. There is always a slight element of going into the unknown when playing *les Bleus* in a match that really matters, and they upped the ante just before the game by spontaneously advancing on the haka.

New Zealand were right to be fearful because for much of the game France seemed to have the upper hand, even if they struggled to find favour with referee Craig Joubert. Every inch on the field was bitterly contested. Although you would never guess from the eventual scoreline, it was probably the best and most compelling World Cup final to date. Just before half-time, Cruden damaged a knee and it was that man Donald, the fourth choice two weeks earlier, who came on and kicked a vital penalty goal to make it 8-7 – the final score, as it happened. New Zealand had scraped home and skipper Richie McCaw, who had defied a nasty ankle ligament injury to guide his team home, gratefully went up to receive the trophy. There was a feeling of redemption and relief among the winners, but the true joy of what they had achieved didn't really surface until they paraded the trophy around Auckland city centre the following afternoon. That trophy tour continued throughout the country for a week or more. As the pre-tournament marketing had foretold, New Zealand was a stadium of four million people and they all wanted to celebrate with their team, in person.

◄ **Brian O'Driscoll won 133 Ireland caps in total** although normally you only get awarded the one on your debut. Ireland, however, also award World Cup caps and BOD has four of those.

▶ **It wasn't a great World Cup for England** and Martin Johnson, on or off the field.

Pool
stages

▼ **Heads bowed, the USA Eagles observe a minute's silence** before their game with Ireland on the tenth anniversary of the 9/11 terrorist atrocity on the Twin Towers. As a 17-year-old college student, Eagles scrum-half Mike Petri was on site almost immediately, delivering oxygen cylinders and heavy-duty cutting gear with his plumber father.

▶ **Mike Tindall cutting a lonely figure** at an England training session.

▼ **US Eagles skipper Todd Clever** adjusts his hair in the heat of battle during their 'Cold War' shoot-out against Russia at Stadium in New Plymouth.

▼ **Russia were making their World Cup debut** and gave a decent account of themselves on the pitch. Off the pitch, some of their fans made a splash as well.

▲ **Tonga get their retaliation in first** against New Zealand with their Sipi Tau haka: 'I have shed my human characteristics,' they chant. 'I drink the ocean and consume the fire. To death or victory my will is fine.' Stirring stuff.

◀ **Death, taxes and Jonny Wilkinson kicking goals** at a World Cup. The England fly-half amassed 277 points in four World Cups. Here he pops over another penalty against Romania.

▶ **England captain Mike Tindall** would rather be anywhere else in the world than at an England press conference having to explain his recent 'run ashore' in Queenstown.

▶ **Big hits are one of the reasons we love the Samoans.** Full-back Paul Williams gets two for the price of one here as he takes on both JP Pietersen and Schalk Burger.

▲ **Samoa weren't quite the force in New Zealand** that some neutrals had hoped but they did find their 'A' game against South Africa in a ferocious pool match at the North Harbour Stadium in Albany. No. 8 George Stowers burrowed over for their try.

▶ **You cannot be serious, ref!** John Smit is too much of a gentleman to utter those immortal words but you just know he is thinking them! Referee Nigel Owens sends him packing for ten minutes for a deliberate knock-on against the Samoans. Smit, of course, believed he was making a genuine attempt at an interception.

▼ **Both Wales and Ireland qualified from the pool stages impressively** and their quarter-final in the 'Cake Tin' in Wellington was much anticipated. Wales made a storming start with a try after three minutes from Shane Williams and never really looked back, running out 22-10 winners.

◀ **We're in the semi-finals, coach.** Skipper Sam Warburton shares the moment with coach Warren Gatland after Wales' quarter-final win over Ireland.

▼ **Australia's 11-9 quarter-final win over South Africa** was a classic backs to the wall effort, built mainly on heroic defence, but when a rare chance to cross the line presented itself, second row and skipper James Horwill accepted with alacrity.

▲ **Israel Dagg was a live wire for New Zealand** throughout the tournament and the semi-final against Australia was no exception. Quade Cooper just about slows him down with a last ditch tap-tackle.

▼ **Wales captain Sam Warbuton** is universally
respected as a fair player player but with the adrenalin
pumping he badly overcooked this tackle on Vincent
Clerc, tipping the French player on his back. Referee
Alain Rolland had no option but to send him off.

◀ **What have I done?** Just 19 minutes into the semi-final against France, Wales' captain Sam Warburton wants the earth to open up and swallow him after being sent off for a 'tip tackle' on Vincent Clerc.

▼ **A penny for his thoughts** as a tearful Warburton looks on as 14-man Wales heroically take the game to France before losing 9-8.

▲ **All the critics were agreed** that the one player Wales couldn't afford to be without against France was prop Adam Jones. As it happened, he hobbled off after just ten minutes with a calf injury.

▼ **France coach Marc Lievremont** seems to be enjoying the last laugh. His team, reportedly disunited and in revolt, had been a shambles for most of the tournament but against the odds they now had a final against New Zealand to prepare for.

The Final

◄ **United at last.** France had been a bickering disparate group for much of the World Cup but they instinctively came together before the final as they advanced as one to face the haka.

▼ **New Zealand, for various reasons, had failed to deliver** since winning the first World Cup in 1987 but were determined to change that. But first came an emotional haka to lay down the challenge to France.

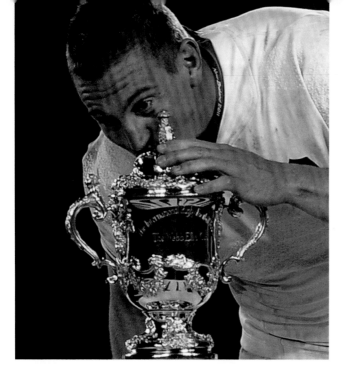

◄ France No. 8 Imanol Harinordoquy clearly isn't superstitious as he stops to kiss the Webb Ellis trophy as he ran out for the final against New Zealand.

▼ We hadn't seen the best of Maxime Médard leading into the final but the Toulouse full-back, known as Wolfman on account of his extravagant sideburns, was back to his best against New Zealand.

▶ France threw the kitchen sink at New Zealand in the final quarter as they trailed 8-7. Replacement Damien Traille challenges Israel Dagg for another high ball.

◀ **New Zealand skipper Richie McCaw** had suffered the disappointment of a semi-final defeat in 2003 and the lowest of lows in Cardiff in 2007 so his quiet satisfaction and pride in 2011 was there for everybody to see.

▶ **New Zealand's enthusiasm for rugby knows no bounds** and found expression every time the All Blacks paraded the World Cup trophy over the coming months.

▼ **Flash mobs doing the haka in the streets** was a feature of RWC 2011. The triumphant All Blacks were the ultimate flash mob as they posed for a picture on the steps of the NZ Parliament building in Wellington and spontaneously let rip.

▷ **Every great New Zealand side earns a nickname** and the class of 2011 were dubbed the 'Unshakeables'. No matter what was thrown their way - the earthquake and consequent disruption before the tournament, injuries to a succession of fly-halves, Richie McCaw playing on one leg at times after damaging a foot and even the emergence of an inspired France team in the final - they remained focused and unshakeable.

8

The Unseen World Cup

Rugby might not yet boast the huge all-embracing qualifying tournaments of the football World Cup, but the fact remains that, historically, over 75 per cent of all Rugby World Cup games have been in qualifying, which was first introduced in a limited form in 1991. This unseen and often unreported aspect of this compelling tournament has its own ambience and stories to tell. For many rugby-playing nations, the reality of 'competing' for a World Cup place is only notional. In effect, what they are doing is contesting their particular division of a continental championship, with the 'blue sky' scenario that one day they will actually find themselves promoted to one of the higher divisions that actually qualifies a team for the World Cup or the repechage process.

Not that it matters. In reality, that very distant goal of a shot at a World Cup is what gives structure and meaning to international rugby way down the ladder, where otherwise the staple diet would be sometimes unsatisfying friendlies with only bragging rights at stake. These matches are a central part of the World Cup odyssey. Under the RWC banner, smaller teams can attract extra media coverage for their game, get local sponsors involved and offer a little romance and glamour for the many amateur players that make up their sides. The IRB makes every effort to ensure the Webb Ellis trophy is seen at many of these far-flung tournaments. This heightens that effect and in a very real way the eclectic, sometimes chaotic qualifying process retains an important link with rugby's touring roots.

The number of available places has differed during the life of the tournament. In 1991 25 nations chased the eight available places, while in 1995 seven of the 16 teams in South Africa were required to qualify, including Ivory Coast, who for the first and only time emerged from the African group.

In 1999, there was a massive departure with only the winners, the beaten finalists, the play-off winners from 1995 and hosts Wales being granted a bye. That resulted in 63 teams chasing a total of 16 places as RWC expanded the Finals to a 20-team

▲ **A little prayer never goes amiss** when taking important kicks. Indeed, the Fijians like to inscribe a little biblical quotation on their custom-made kicking tees. For those of you wondering: 'Some trust in chariots and some in horses, but we trust in the name of the Lord our God'.

◀ **For some, happiness** will always be a good scrum. These youngsters from Madagascar are getting in the mood at the African World Cup qualifying tournament in Antananarivo in 2014.

format. As a consequence, there were many extremely one-sided qualification ties. Of course, there were also some startling games as well, notably England just scraping home 23-15 against Italy at Huddersfield, when Italy's scrum-half Alessandro Troncon had what looked like a fair try disallowed. For Australia in 2003 the format changed again, with the eight quarter-finalists from 1999 going straight through, leaving 12 teams required to pre-qualify. For 2007, 2011 and 2015 the system has finally settled with the top three teams in each pool from the preceding World Cup granted byes, while the rest of the world chases the remaining eight places. In 2011, 96 nations were involved in the process at some stage, while for 2015 the number is 92. That's a lot of rugby.

Far-flung chronicles

I've found myself in some pretty far-flung parts of the rugby world chronicling the qualifying process. Krasnoyarsk in deepest Siberia probably tops the list, a rarely visited and strangely exotic venue that assaulted all the senses. This true rugby stronghold welcomed anybody visiting for the 'match' – which in my case was Ireland's World Cup qualifier against Russia.

We left Dublin at breakfast time on Thursday and returned to Ireland on Sunday afternoon, having crossed 14 time zones there and back in what amounted to a smash and grab raid halfway around the globe. Arriving at 2 a.m. local time, via Moscow, the Ireland party was met by no less than seven TV crews, all of whom barged their way past numerous Ireland players in search of captain 'Keef Woodie', who was clearly huge in that part of the world. Contrary to preconceptions of Siberia, the sun was cracking rocks during our short stay as temperatures soared into the high 80s. Winter arrived and the snow started falling, as it always does apparently, on 25 September, three days after our departure.

There is no autumn apparently in Krasnoyarsk, a real rugby citadel where two of Russia's Super Ten sides play. In the depths of winter the players train in the famed underground city of Krasnoyarsk 26, which was built at the height of the Cold War and boasts cavernous hangar space capable of housing hundreds of aircraft. Indeed, many are still mothballed there, but there is more than enough spare capacity for full-scale rugby practices in the most controlled of environments while the Siberian winter rages outside.

Taking our cue from the Ireland playing squad, camp followers stayed on Irish time for the duration. This meant the blistering early

Saturday morning sun was just beginning to rise as we enjoyed our 'quiet' Friday night beer in one of the scores of Country and Western bars that adorn downtown Krasnoyarsk, and which are conveniently open 24-7. While we all ate an early breakfast, the locals were tucking into a late lunch.

The match was played in the heat of late afternoon in an atmospheric stadium situated on an island in the middle of the Yenisei River with a colourful picnic scene in the car park outside. Latecomers who missed the national anthem, however, were locked out. The huge doors to the stadium shut just before the anthem started up and didn't open again until half-time. Ireland won a highly physical encounter 32-3 and, after being lavishly entertained that night, headed straight home the following morning.

Riga in 1996 was another interesting trip, with the Latvians kicking off the qualifying process for the 1999 World Cup with a game against Norway. It was early spring and still bitterly cold, but both sets of players were coming out of their winter hibernation, when playing rugby really is a challenge. In Latvia, they actually run a winter league of snow rugby in which they mark out the snowbound pitch with wood chippings from the many local sawmills. A hardy lot, but typical of tens of thousands of rugby players across the globe. Paddy Whelan's Irish Bar is their unofficial clubhouse, where they display all their memorabilia, and that is where they marched us to celebrate their 44-6 victory.

The rugby folk of Romania were no different as they tried to deal with the chaos and poverty of the Ceaușescu regime in the early 1990s. My distinct memory of a qualifying match in Bucharest against Wales in 1994 is not of the sweltering 90-degree heat in the furnace of a national stadium, which coach Alan Davies

described as life-threatening, but of the post-match 'banquet' at a ramshackle hotel. It soon became quite obvious that the Romanian players and officials on my table were hardly eating any of the cold meats laid out and most certainly were not drinking the wine provided. So scarce were such 'luxuries' that they were under strict instructions to let their visitors tuck in first and only join the feast if there was anything left. Happily, the Wales squad soon picked up on this and ensured that whatever was available was shared out equally between everyone.

That ability to compete and play host in the face of all sorts of adversity never ceases to amaze me. This was brought home to me starkly when I visited Antananarivo in Madagascar in July 2014 for the CAR Africa 1 championships, which doubled up on this occasion as the African World Cup qualifying tournament. By any criteria, Madagascar is a poor country – some WHO statistics suggest it's the fourth poorest on the planet – yet against all the odds the local federation worked tirelessly to lay on a superb competition, which went off without a hitch in testing conditions.

Such occasions are Madagascar's World Cup final. A rugby-mad nation that will always struggle physically to live with the very

◄ **The Webb Ellis trophy.** Purchased from Garrards of London for £6,000 shortly before the 1987 tournament.

▼ **Rugby is predominantly a winter game ...** but not in the Caribbean! The Cayman and Trinidad & Tobago captains pose for publicity shots before the Caribbean qualifying tournament held on Grand Cayman in April 2008.

best, that is still no impediment to being the best they can be on and off the field. The arrival of the World Cup trophy on the island was a huge event, celebrated at numerous schools and isolated hamlets in the hills, but it was also the conduit for so much else. Madagascan TV, for example, presented its main breakfast-time news programme from the national stadium every match day, using the rugby tournament as its backdrop.

These World Cup qualifiers magnify what I like most about rugby. Andorra's hosting of Norway in 2004, the first qualifying game of the 2007 World Cup, was another case in point. The Andorrans were a glorious mix of locals, an itinerant Aussie ski instructor and several Georgian nightclub bouncers who had arrived in the Pyrenees ten years earlier and liked it so much they stayed and took nationality. They were actually very competitive that year and disposed of Norway in short order, but then the real event of the weekend got underway.

Not only did they show the Norwegian lads all that Andorra la Vella had to offer, after the last nightclub had closed, they headed

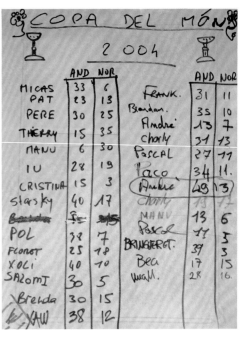

◄▲ **The 2007 World Cup** actually kicked off in Andorra in September 2004 with the home team taking on Norway in a match refereed by Andre Watson who was the South African official who took charge of the 2003 World Cup Final. At the club's local Bar Tequilla they ran a sweepstake on the result, Andre winning E54 for his 49-13 prediction. Andorra actually won 76-13.

▶ **Uruguay captain Diego Ormaechea** celebrates qualifying for the 1999 finals after beating Morocco in a two-legged play-off game. Ormaechea was 40 when he represented Uruguay in the pool games and his son Agustin Ormaechea, barring injury, will be playing for Los Teros at RWC 2015.

for the hills and an annual fiesta where the partying is extreme. It was the best part of a week later that some of the Norwegians made it back home. Neither nation will ever reach the finals of the World Cup, but very few will derive more pleasure from the competition and have more fun. Even in its full professional maturity the Rugby World Cup still manages to retain the essential spirit of the game and doff its hat to the old amateur days and ways. That is some conjuring trick.

The power of the actual trophy is considerable and should never be underestimated. It was purchased in haste and many consider it undersized – it can look like a wine goblet when giants like Martin Johnson or John Eales take hold of it – but in my opinion it is one of sport's more beautiful and seductive trophies. It already has an enviable history. This is the trophy, after all, that helped change a nation – South Africa – and was brandished by Mandela himself. That impression was reinforced during a visit to the Cayman Islands in 2009 for the start of the Caribbean qualifying tournament for 2011. Life is pretty relaxed in that well-heeled paradise and one morning Getty Images photographer David Rogers and I took the shiny gold-plate cup – Bill, as it is known in certain circles – for an impromptu stroll down Seven Mile Beach. Probably not one sunbather in 20 had any idea what the trophy was, but they instantly

formed a long queue to be photographed alongside it. The William Webb Ellis Cup has the undeniable X-factor.

The tournament continues to grow apace. Over 2.2 million spectators will be attending the 48 games at RWC 2015 where many of the games, judging from online ticket application, could have been sold out three or four times over. The World Cup has undeniably come a long way. In a very real way the doomsayers were correct, it did sound the death knell of amateurism at the elite level, but equally it has quickly become the main financial driver and cash cow of the professional game. Rugby union needed to go professional, it had reached a tipping point and a well-run and globally recognised Rugby World Cup has played an important and stabilising role in the process.

Miraculously, through those early rounds and the continuing endeavours of the weekend warriors for the minnow nations, the World Cup has nonetheless retained a vital connection with the old amateur game and its ethos. The spirit lives on. It's not perfect – you still wonder why a tournament hosted by England, which now boasts some of the best sports stadia in the world, is staging eight high-profile matches in Wales – but the fact remains that it is impossible to envisage the modern day rugby landscape without the Rugby World Cup.

▲ **The Namibian squad drop on their knees** in prayer after qualifying for WC 2015 in dramatic style at the African qualifying group with a commanding win over hosts Madagascar. Their coach Danie Vermeulen is in the wheelchair.

◄ **Humphrey Kayange**, one of Kenya's leading lawyers outside of rugby, skips through for a try in the World Cup qualifier against Zimbabwe.

▶ **The sun never sets** on the rugby world these days! The Caymans take on Mexico in a World Cup qualifier.

A picture that sums up why many of us love rugby. Namibia's warrior flanker Tinus du Plessis celebrates helping his team qualify for RWC 2015.

The arrival of a World Cup qualifying tournament is a good chance to fly the rugby flag in developing rugby nations. In Madagascar last year, coaching clinics were held in inner city regions of Antananarivo while the World Cup itself was taken to the famous Don Pedro school on the city outskirts where the Maki - Madagascar's national team - dropped in to spend a day with the pupils.

◀ **Georgia are always formidable** at the national stadium Tbilisi and a capacity 50,000 crowd were there to cheer them on in November 2013 to see them qualify for RWC 2015 with a hard-fought win over bitter rivals Russia.

▶ **Fiji against the Cook Islands** in Suva. Now there's a fixture to ponder on!

▶ **England have only had to qualify once** for the World Cup, when they had to play Holland and Italy in 1998. The Dutch were hammered but the Italians, inspired by Diego Dominguez at fly-half, produced a fine performance at the McAlpine Stadium Huddersfield and, despite being denied a perfectly legitimate try, only lost 23-15.

2015 Pools

POOL A TEAMS	
1	Australia
2	England
3	Wales
4	Fiji
5	Uruguay

POOL B TEAMS	
1	South Africa
2	Samoa
3	Japan
4	Scotland
5	USA

POOL C TEAMS	
1	New Zealand
2	Argentina
3	Tonga
4	Georgia
5	Namibia

POOL D TEAMS	
1	France
2	Ireland
3	Italy
4	Canada
5	Romania

Statistics

Year	Host(s)	FINAL			BRONZE FINAL			No. of teams	Top Points Scorer	Top Try Scorer	Winning Coach	Winning Captain	Total Attendance
		Winner	Score	Runners-up	3rd place	Score	4th Place						
1987	Australia & New Zealand	New Zealand	29–9	France	Wales	22–21	Australia	16	Grant Fox, New Zealand (126)	Craig Green, New Zealand (6) John Kirwan, New Zealand (6)	Brian Lochore	David Kirk	604,500
1991	England, Wales, France, Ireland, Scotland	Australia	12–6	England	New Zealand	13–6	Scotland	16	Ralph Keyes, Ireland (68)	David Campese, Australia (6) Jean-Baptiste Lafond, France (6)	Bob Dwyer	Nick Farr-Jones	1,007,760
1995	South Africa	South Africa	15–12 (aet)	New Zealand	France	19–9	England	16	Thierry Lacroix, France (112)	Jonah Lomu, New Zealand (7) Marc Ellis, New Zealand (7)	Kitch Christie	Francois Pienaar	1,100,000
1999	Wales	Australia	35–12	France	South Africa	22–18	New Zealand	20	Gonzalo Quesada, Argentina (102)	Jonah Lomu, New Zealand (8)	Rod Macqueen	John Eales	1,750,000
2003	Australia	England	20–17 (aet)	Australia	New Zealand	40–13	France	20	Jonny Wilkinson, England (11)	Doug Howlett, New Zealand (7) Mils Muliaina, New Zealand (7)	Clive Woodward	Martin Johnson	1,837,547
2007	France	South Africa	15–6	England	Argentina	34–10	France	20	Percy Montgomery, South Africa (105)	Bryan Habana, South Africa (8)	Jake White	John Smit	2,263,223
2011	New Zealand	New Zealand	8–7	France	Australia	21–18	Wales	20	Morné Steyn, South Africa (62)	Chris Ashton, England (6) Vincent Clerc, France (6)	Graham Henry	Richie McCaw	1,477,294
2015	England							20					

Index

Photo credits

All images © Getty Images with the exception of the following; p. 212 © Frank Coppi

Acknowledgements

The great pleasure in completing a book like this is trawling through the massive Getty archive to select some 300 images that hopefully convey something of the magic and the story of Rugby World Cup over the years. If I started again tomorrow it would be perfectly possible to pick another 300 images altogether and tell the same story, such is the variety and quality of the pictures available.

A collective acknowledgment to all those Getty staff men and stringers is a 'given'; but as they are among the most talented professionals I have encountered – and barely get a word of public acknowledgement in their everyday working lives – this is the perfect opportunity to mention as many as possible by name. Alas some of the pictures simply went under the generic Getty by-line and it was not possible to easily discern the man behind the lens in all cases so apologies in advance to anybody inadvertently missed out.

In no particular order I give you David Rogers, Ross Kinnard, Alex Livesey, Shaun Botterill, Russell Cheyne, Simon Bruty, Mike Hewitt, Mark Leech, Phil Cole, Clive Mason, Mike Brett, Gerry Bernard, Ross Setford, Georges Gobet and Gabriel Bouys – as strong a XV, in their own way, as you will find anywhere in the world of rugby.

I have been lucky enough to work closely with a number of those named and have looked on in awe at the seemingly effortless ease and modesty that always accompanies their labours. Not that they don't have their moments of stress as they cope with every weather known to man, grapple with ridiculous deadlines like the rest of us and try to keep their cool when jobsworths the world over seem hell-bent on preventing them from earning a living.

Simply being at the right place at the right time with the right lens – day after day for months on end – is a major accomplishment in its own right even before they even snap a shot in anger. Their 'reports' from the battle front and endless behind the scenes gossip – if you want to know what's really happening always ask a snapper – are great value in the late night bars they are known to occasionally frequent and one day I will write that book as well.

I know for a fact that one of the most iconic shots of all from the 1987 Cup Final, in those pre-digital days, and included in this book was the only image of a film of 24 frames that came out. Some sort of flash malfunction allegedly! And the gentleman concerned was taking that 'money shot' for the entire press gang as, nominally rivals but showing exemplary teamwork, they split up to ensure coverage of every angle of proceedings.

Another shot in this book, in the 2011 section, was taken by a photographer who just half an hour earlier had painfully broken his ankle but pressed on regardless. The 1991 chapter features a picture from a photographer who had broken his arm when slipping up napping the teams singing the anthems. The heroics are not just confined to the field of play. Thanks also to Frank Coppi, another redoubtable snapper, for his pictures from our memorable trip to Andorra.

Talking of professionalism and getting the job done – although hopefully without either a broken leg or arm – it would be remiss also not to doff my cap to Sarah Cole who has edited this project with a Jonny Wilkinson-like calm and tenacity. Many thanks Sarah and also Kirsty Schaper at Bloomsbury who commissioned the project and whose early enthusiasm was so important in getting it up and running.

Brendan Gallagher *May 2015*